How to use your Snap Revision Text Guide

This 'Unseen Poetry' Snap Revision Guide wil[l]
unseen poetry section of your AQA English L[iterature]
sections so you can easily find help with diffe[rent]
This book covers everything you will need to

s.

Approach to poetry: how to analyse unseen [poetry, with sample]
analysis, quick questions and exam practice i[n]

Comparison: how to come up with ideas and structure a comparison of two poems.

The exam: what kind of questions will come up in the exam, how you can get top
marks, and what grade 5 and grade 7+ responses look like.

To help you get ready for your exam, each topic includes:

Summary
The key skills to practise as you prepare for the exam.

Sample analysis
An example of the kind of analysis that the examiner will be looking for.

Questions to consider
Develop your approach to new poetry.

Quick test
A quick-fire test to check you can remember the main points about each poem.

Exam practice
A short writing task so you can practise analysing each poem.

Glossary
A handy list of literary terms, with easy-to-understand definitions, that you will find
useful when revising unseen poetry.

QR Codes

Found throughout the
book, the QR codes can
be scanned on your
smartphone and link to
a video working through
the solution to the Exam
Practice question on each
topic, plus selected poetry
recitals.

AUTHOR:
STEVE
EDDY

ebook

To access the ebook, visit
collins.co.uk/ebooks
and follow the step-by-step
instructions.

ACKNOWLEDGEMENTS

The author and publisher are grateful to the copyright holders for permission to use quoted materials and images.

Every effort has been made to trace copyright holders and obtain their permission for the use of copyright material. The author and publisher will gladly receive information enabling them to rectify any error or omission in subsequent editions. All facts are correct at time of going to press.

p.5-6, 'Epitaph for a Wood-Turner' by Steve Eddy, reproduced by permission of Steve Eddy; p.8, 'Darling & Me!', taken from: *Look We Have Coming to Dover!* by Daljit Nagra © 2007 Daljit Nagra. Used by permission of Faber and Faber; p.12, 'A Small Girl Swinging' by George Szirtes, reproduced by permission of George Szirtes; p.14, 'Traffic' by Billy Collins, from The Rain in Portugal, reproduced by permission of Picador through PLSclear; p.15-16, 'A Cry from the Blue' by Shaun McCarthy, reproduced by permission of Shaun McCarthy; p.16-17, 'Hollow' by Vanessa Kisuule, © Vanessa Kisuule. Granted with permission on behalf of the author by Lewinsohn Literary Agency Ltd; p.20-21, 'The Thief of Love' by Sheenagh Pugh, reproduced by permission of Seren Books; p.24, 'R.A.P.' taken from: *Bloodshot Monochrome* by Patience Agbabi. Published by Canongate Books. © 2008 Patience Agbabi. Cleared through PLS Clear; p.25, 'White Van Man' by Gillian Penrose, reproduced by permission of Gillian Penrose; p.26, 'Close Encounters III' by Raman Mundair; p.28-29, 'Being Dead' by Paul Matthews, from This Naked Light (2018) published by Troubador Books, reproduced by permission of Paul Matthews; p.30, 'In My Country' taken from: *Out of Bounds: British Black & Asian Poets* by Jackie Kay, © 2012 Jackie Kay. Reproduced by permission of Bloodaxe Books; p.38, 'The Trick' taken from: *Luck is the Hook* by Imtiaz Dharker. © 2018 Imtiaz Dharker. Used by permission of Bloodaxe Books; p.41, 'Bell Ringers' by Matthew Barton, from Vessel (2009), reproduced by permission of Matthew Barton; p.42, 'Campanologists' by Paul Groves, reproduced by permission of Seren Books; p.46, 'Nile Kingfisher' by Steve Eddy, reproduced by permission of Steve Eddy; p.47, 'Tench' by Steve Eddy, reproduced by permission of Steve Eddy; p.50-51, 'Fall Snow' by Matthew Barton, from Family Tree (2016), reproduced by permission of Matthew Barton and Shoestring Press; p.52, 'Reggae Head' taken from: *Propa Propaganda* by: Benjamin Zephaniah. © 1996 Benjamin Zephaniah. Used by permission of Bloodaxe Book; p.56, 'Long Ago' by Douglas Dunn, reproduced by permission of Faber & Faber Ltd; p.65, 'Night Ferry' by George Szirtes, reproduced by permission of George Szirtes; p.65-66, 'House on a Cliff' by Louis MacNeice, from Collected Poems, Faber & Faber Ltd.

Published by Collins
An imprint of HarperCollins*Publishers*
1 London Bridge Street
London SE1 9GF

HarperCollins*Publishers*
1st Floor, Watermarque Building, Ringsend Road, Dublin 4, Ireland

© HarperCollins*Publishers* Limited 2022

ISBN 9780008551568

First published 2022

10 9 8 7 6 5 4 3 2 1

British Library Cataloguing in Publication Data.

A CIP record of this book is available from the British Library.

Commissioning Editors: Gillian Bowman and Clare Souza
Managing Editors: Craig Balfour and Shelley Teasdale
Author: Steve Eddy
Proofreaders: Jill Laidlaw and Fiona Watson
Typesetting: QBS Learning
Cover designers: Kneath Associates and Sarah Duxbury
Production: Molly McNevin
Printed in the United Kingdom by Martins the Printers.

MIX
Paper from
responsible sources
FSC
www.fsc.org
FSC™ C007454

Contents

Aspects of poetry

In your exam you will have to answer two questions on 'unseen poetry' – poems that you will probably not have read before. You will have had no chance to revise these. However, it *is* possible to learn, and practise, a method by which to analyse *any* poem.

This method consists of identifying the different elements outlined in this section, and commenting on whichever are most relevant to the poem. You will see that the elements can be memorised using the mnemonic sentence 'What Voice Forms Language?', where each word in the sentence is an element: 'What (is it about)', 'Voice', 'Forms' and 'Language'.

What is it about? Subject, theme and narrative

The first question to ask is – What is the poem about? (What is its subject?) The title may shed light on this, if it is more than just the first line repeated. It may tell you exactly what the poem is about, but it may not be that straightforward. Take the following poem by Anne Brontë:

Night

I love the silent hour of night,
    For blissful dreams may then arise,
Revealing to my charmèd sight
    What may not bless my waking eyes.

And then a voice may meet my ear,
    That death has silenced long ago;
And hope and rapture may appear
    Instead of solitude and woe.

Cold in the grave for years has lain
    The form it was my bliss to see;
And only dreams can bring again
    The darling of my heart to me.

This is, as the title suggests, partly about night, but it quickly becomes apparent that it is what happens at night that matters to the speaker: she dreams of someone she has loved and lost. So, you could say that the poem is about dreams consoling the bereaved.

Looking further into the ideas behind the poem, its **themes** could include death, longing and imagination.

Some poems are **narrative**: they tell a story. 'Night' tells no obvious story, but it does imply a simple narrative: the speaker has lost a loved one; she is now lonely, but her grief is relieved by dreams.

Voice, viewpoint, tone and mood

Voice

A poem's **voice** is the person or character whom we imagine speaking. We cannot assume that this is simply the poet speaking directly to the reader, as sometimes the poet adopts a particular attitude for effect, so it is safer to write about 'the speaker'. For example:

> In 'Night' the speaker is consoled by dreams of a lost loved one.

Some poems are written in character – adopting a **persona**, as in W. B. Yeats' poem 'An Irish Airman Foresees his Death':

> I know that I shall meet my fate
>
> Somewhere among the clouds above;
>
> Those that I fight I do not hate,
>
> Those that I guard I do not love;

Viewpoint (perspective)

This largely refers to whether the poem is written in the first person, like the two poems above, the second person (addressing someone as 'you'), or the third person, like the short **epitaph** poem below:

> **Epitaph for a Wood-Turner**
>
> He thought that he had been quite clever
>
> carving a career, making his mark.
>
> Turns out he was only ever
>
> whittling in the dark.

However, it is possible for a poet to write in the third person but still convey the attitude and character of an imagined speaker by writing in the kind of language they might use.

Tone and mood

These elements are closely related. **Tone** refers to how the poet addresses the reader – for example, in a conversational tone, or a bitter tone. In 'Epitaph for a Wood-Turner', the tone is darkly humorous, joking about the wood-turner 'whittling' (a **pun** on 'whistling') in the dark. This pun on a colloquial expression also makes the tone conversational.

Mood has more to do with a poem's overall emotional effect, though in a long poem, the mood may develop as the poem progresses. The mood of Anne Brontë's 'Night' is one of sadness mixed with hope. Words like 'blissful', 'charmèd' and 'rapture' contrast with 'solitude and woe', and 'Cold in the grave'.

Forms and structure

The **form** of a poem refers to its verse patterns and how it is divided into **stanzas**.

Verse patterns (prosody)

A poem could be in a **metre** – a pattern of lines consisting of a certain number of stressed and unstressed syllables. In both Anne Brontë's 'Night' and Yeats' 'An Irish Airman Foresees his Death', each line is composed of four pairs of syllables. Each pair consists of an unstressed syllable, followed by a stressed syllable:

> I <u>love</u> / the <u>si</u> / lent <u>hour</u> / of <u>night</u>

> I <u>know</u> / that <u>I</u> / shall <u>meet</u> / my <u>fate</u>

You will not earn many marks just by identifying the metre. However, good poets emphasise meaning by subtly varying the metre. For example, if you read 'Night' aloud, you should find that it moves along smoothly in a 'di-dum, di-dum …' rhythm until you reach this line:

> Cold in the grave for years has lain

Sticking to the rhythm here would stress the word 'in', but it sounds more natural, and makes more sense, to stress 'Cold'. This, however, breaks the rhythm, drawing attention to the word and adding to its impact. Read the poem aloud to hear this yourself.

Form also includes **rhyme**, which is often used with metre to create pattern. The Brontë and Yeats poems have the same **rhyme scheme**. Line 1 rhymes with line 3; line 2 rhymes with line 4. Rhyme schemes are identified using letters: this would be called an *abab* rhyme scheme – the first line rhymes with the third, the second with the fourth, and so on.

Again, you will not earn many marks just by pointing this out, but you will earn marks for explaining why it is appropriate, and how it is used to emphasise particular words. For example, Anne Brontë rhymes 'night' with 'sight', underlining the paradox that she 'sees' better in the dark.

Stanzas

A poem may be set out as one paragraph, or it may be split into stanzas. In a metrical poem, each stanza may be a basic unit of metre, with the metrical pattern being repeated in each stanza. Just as with prose paragraphing, the poet may introduce a new idea in each new stanza, or a new development of the main theme.

Structure

This refers to the development of the poet's ideas. In a narrative poem, this may relate closely to the story. In a poem without a strong narrative, it may relate to the development of the poem's mood. Or the poet may describe an event or scene and then draw a conclusion from it.

Language

Poets choose words in order to achieve particular effects. The poet Samuel Taylor Coleridge called poetry 'the best words in the best order'. For example, look again at the start of Yeats' poem:

> I know that I shall meet my fate
> Somewhere among the clouds above

He could have written, 'I know that I shall meet my death', but this would not have carried the same sense of his being resigned to the inevitable. Similarly, his use of 'among the clouds', rather than 'up in the sky', conveys a sense of mystery and uncertainty.

Connotations

The impact of individual words is influenced by what readers associate with them – their **connotations**. For example, Yeats uses the word 'clouds'. What ideas do you associate with clouds? This is up to you to explain. You might, for example, write:

> The speaker's use of 'clouds' suggests a sense of mystery about how he will die.

On the other hand, clouds can be associated with trouble, so there could be a deliberate **ambiguity** in Yeats' use of the word. Language can have layers of meaning, and alternative interpretations. There is no single 'correct' interpretation of a poem. Showing that you are aware of this will add depth to your commentaries on poems.

Imagery

Imagery uses comparison to create a word picture:

- **metaphors** speak of something as if it *is* something else, as in 'carving a career', which speaks of a career as if it were a piece of wood
- **similes** compare one thing with another more explicitly, using 'like', 'as' or 'than'
- **personification** is a special type of metaphor describing an abstract idea, such as love or time, as if it were a person or a god; for example, the following lines personify time as a charioteer:

> But at my back I always hear
> Time's wingèd chariot hurrying near
>
> *Andrew Marvell, 'To his Coy Mistress'*

Sound effects

The sounds of words also help to shape their meaning. The principal sound effects are:

- **alliteration** – the repetition of consonant (non-vowel) sounds at the beginnings of words or stressed syllables (e.g. '<u>c</u>arving a <u>c</u>areer, <u>m</u>aking his <u>m</u>ark')
- **assonance** – the repetition of vowel sounds (e.g. 'c<u>a</u>rving ... m<u>a</u>rk')
- **onomatopoeia** – the use of words that sound like what they mean (e.g. 'buzz')
- **sibilance** – the use of words that make a hissing sound (e.g. 'whisper').

The poet Daljit Nagra uses these techniques to great effect in his poem 'Darling & Me!'.

> Di barman's bell done dinging
> so I phone di dimply-mississ,
> *Putting some gas on cookah,*
> *bonus pay I bringin!*
> Downing drink, I giddily
> home for Pakeezah record
> to which we go-go, tango,
> for roti—to kitchen—she rumba!

Pakeezah: Indian romantic musical film
go-go: type of party music and dance
tango, rumba: types of dance
roti: Indian flatbread

Ask yourself

- How is onomoatopeia used in the first line?
- What mood is created by the alliteration and assonance?
- How does rhythm combine with alliteration to create a party mood?

Summary

- Poems can be analysed by examining their key elements:
  - **What** they are about (subject, themes and narrative)
  - **Voice**, viewpoint, tone and mood
  - **Forms** (including metre, stanzas and rhyme) and structure
  - **Language** (including word choices, imagery and sound effects)
- These elements can be remembered using the mnemonic sentence 'What Voice Forms Language?'

Sample analysis

'Night' contrasts the 'love', 'bliss', 'hope' and 'rapture' that the speaker feels in her dreams with the awful sense of 'solitude and woe' that she feels when awake, because she has lost a loved one. The smoothly flowing **iambic** rhythm conveys her positive feelings while dreaming, but these are interrupted with shocking impact by the rhythmic change that comes with 'Cold in the grave', where sense requires the emphasis to be on 'Cold' rather than 'in'. This gives a sense of the grave bringing life to a sudden halt.

Questions

QUICK TEST
1. What is the difference between the subject of a poem and its themes?
2. What word is used for a set rhythmic pattern in a poem?
3. Which type of image uses 'like', 'as' or 'than'?

EXAM PRACTICE
Write a paragraph commenting on the three-stanza structure of 'Night'.

What is it about? How Subject Relates to Theme

In most cases, the best thing to comment on first is what the poem seems to be about – its subject. With older poems, like the one below by William Wordsworth, this may be fairly obvious. Here are some typical types of subject:

- a character, dead or alive, and perhaps what they mean, or meant, to the poet
- an event – perhaps in the poet's life, or a historical event
- a place and its significance or atmosphere
- an animal and its nature.

Read the poem below and consider what it is about.

She Dwelt among the Untrodden Ways

She dwelt among the untrodden ways
Beside the springs of Dove,
A Maid whom there were none to praise
And very few to love:

A violet by a mossy stone
Half hidden from the eye!
—Fair as a star, when only one
Is shining in the sky.

She lived unknown, and few could know
When Lucy ceased to be;
But she is in her grave, and, oh,
The difference to me!

Asking yourself questions

Don't worry if you don't understand everything in the poem straight away. You could probably work out that this poem is about 'Lucy', a girl or young woman known to the poet or his imagined speaker, that she has died, and that he misses her. The fact that she has died makes it an **elegy**. To say more about the subject, and to explore its themes, you would have to ask yourself some questions, and start to look for evidence in the poem with which to answer them:

* What is meant by 'untrodden ways', and how is it significant that she lived there?
* How well-known was she? Was she a popular girl, adored by her many friends and family members?
* According to the speaker, what was Lucy like, and what images show this?
* How does the speaker feel about her death, and how is this revealed?

You also have to look for what is *implied* – for example, by Lucy living in a remote place.

Themes

Remember that a poem's themes are the big ideas behind its apparent subject matter. These could include, for example, love, money, loss or childhood. Most good poems explore themes rather than making a fixed statement with just one interpretation. Be aware, too, that the language choices contribute to the themes, not just the story or apparent meaning of the words.

So, in this poem, some possible themes based on the questions above are:

* Innocence – Lucy lived 'among the untrodden ways', meaning far from towns or villages, by the source of the river Dove, whose name is a symbol of peace.
* The natural goodness of someone brought up surrounded by nature. Wordsworth uses nature imagery to describe her – the metaphor of a violet, a small, beautiful flower that can grow in partial shade, and a simile comparing her with a star.
* Virtue that goes unnoticed. Lucy 'lived unknown' and few were aware of her death.
* Personal loss. The speaker's feelings are conveyed simply by the exclamation, 'oh, / The difference to me!'.

Poems with a less obvious subject

Now read the modern poem on the next page. The subject has something in common with Wordsworth's poem, and its language suggests childhood innocence. Yet what it is really about is open to interpretation. If you write about a poem like this, you are not expected to give a full explanation but should suggest possible meanings or ideas. However, you do need to back up your ideas with evidence from the text.

Read the poem a second time, thinking about the annotations and how they might help you to comment on its subject and themes. Making your own annotations on a poem in this way will help you to engage with it.

A Small Girl Swinging

When first they pushed me
      I was very scared.
My tummy jiggled. I was
      Unprepared.

The second time was higher
      And my ears
Were cold with whisperings
      Of tiny fears.

The third time it was HIGH,
      My teeth on edge.
My heart leapt off the bedroom
      Window-ledge.

The fourth time, Oh, the fourth time
      It was mad.
My skirt flew off the world
      And I was glad.

No one's pushing now,
      My ears are ringing.
Who'll see across the park
      A small girl swinging?

Who'll hear across the park
      Her mother calling,
And everywhere her shadows
      Rising, falling?

George Szirtes

Annotations:
- Who? [→ they]
- Childish language for fear. [→ My tummy jiggled. I was]
- Effect? Who or what is whispering? [→ whisperings]
- Effect of capitals? [→ HIGH]
- Excited or terrified? [→ My heart leapt off]
- Changed attitude; simple rhyme linking 'glad' to 'mad'. [→ And I was glad.]
- What implied? Has she been abandoned? [→ No one's pushing now,]
- Night approaching? Menace? [→ shadows]

Summary

- Typical subjects are a character, an event or a significant place.
- To explore subject and themes, ask yourself questions and look for what is implied.
- Themes are the big ideas explored in a poem.
- You are not expected to give full, clear-cut explanations of poems.

Sample analysis

There is a sense of uncertainty throughout 'A Small Girl Swinging', especially in its narrative. At first sight it seems clear: stanza 1 is about the first time the girl was pushed, stanza 2 about the second time, and so on. However, the reader is left to wonder who the pronoun 'they' refers to, and later, how the girl continues to swing when 'No one's pushing'. Also, the narrative cannot be taken literally. The girl's heart cannot be on the 'bedroom window-ledge', though the detail implies that she is thinking of being safe at home. Similarly, her skirt cannot literally fly 'off the world': this may be a childish expression of her excited sense of expanding horizons.

Questions

QUICK TEST

1. Which of these could *not* be a theme? Choose from: time, childhood, swinging, family, fear.

2. What should you always include if you suggest interpretations for what a poem is about?

3. What themes can you identify in 'She Dwelt among the Untrodden Ways'?

4. How would you describe the girl's feelings at the end of 'A Small Girl Swinging'?

EXAM PRACTICE

Write a paragraph commenting on how the mood of 'A Small Girl Swinging' develops over the course of the poem.

'A Small Girl Swinging' in the previous section tells a story but does not necessarliy describe real events. Nonetheless it implies a narrative of changing feelings, from childish fear, to exhilaration, to a sense of threat. Many narrative poems are more realistic than this. There are also narrative poems in which little happens; this may even be their point.

Narrative making a point

Some poems tell a story to make a point. Sometimes the poet tells a story and then comments on its meaning. In the poem below, the poet builds up details of what happens while he is in a traffic jam. How do the details create a sense of time passing?

Traffic

A child on a silver bicycle,

a young mother pushing a stroller,

and a runner who looked like he was
running to Patagonia

> **Patagonia** – remote area on the southern tip of South America.

have all passed my car, jammed

into a traffic jam on a summer weekend.

And now an elderly couple gradually

overtakes me as does a family of snails –

me stalled as if in a pit of tar

far from any beach and its salty air.

Why even Buddha has risen

from his habitual sitting

> **Buddha** – religious figure associated with calm and patient meditation.

and is now walking serenely past my car,

holding his robes to his chest with one hand.

I watch him from the patch of shade

I have inched into as he begins to grow smaller

over my steering wheel then sits down again

up ahead, unfurling his palms

as if he were only a tiny figurine affixed to the dash.

Billy Collins

Questions to consider

- At what point do the details become unrealistic, and what is the effect?
- What does the third stanza suggest about the poet's feelings, and where he might be going?
- Why does he introduce the Buddha?
- What is the effect of the final image?

How poets comment on narrative

In 'Traffic', the poet makes no comment on his narrative. Some poems, however, tell a story and then explore its meaning.

Whereas 'Traffic' was about time passing slowly, with the speaker only able to observe the evidence, 'A Cry from the Blue', below, seems to be about a single moment in time, when the speaker's lawnmower has stalled. The poet describes it, then considers its significance.

Both poems are about time and place. In 'Traffic', the poet is stuck in one place; in 'A Cry from the Blue', the speaker is intensely aware of his surroundings at a particular moment. In both, narrative is linked to structure.

'A Cry from the Blue' begins with a narrative convention, setting the scene: time and weather, then location.

A Cry from the Blue

It was the middle afternoon,
hot and stinging, when suddenly
there was a cry from the blue,   ← Unexpected and urgent.
grounded in no one place.

The field beyond the hedge was still,
nothing slipped round the green corner
and all points held the slight
surprise of inanimate objects   ← Personifies inanimate things – projecting own experience onto them?
disturbed, in their essence, by humans.

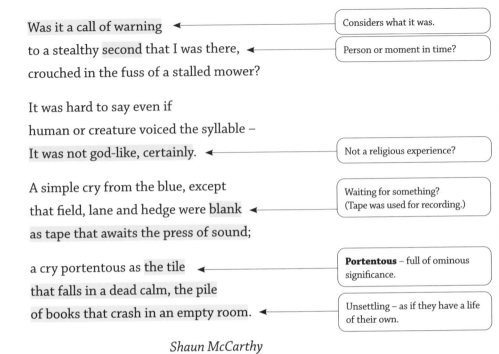

Was it a call of warning
to a stealthy second that I was there,
crouched in the fuss of a stalled mower?

It was hard to say even if
human or creature voiced the syllable –
It was not god-like, certainly.

A simple cry from the blue, except
that field, lane and hedge were blank
as tape that awaits the press of sound;

a cry portentous as the tile
that falls in a dead calm, the pile
of books that crash in an empty room.

Shaun McCarthy

Annotations:
- Considers what it was.
- Person or moment in time?
- Not a religious experience?
- Waiting for something? (Tape was used for recording.)
- **Portentous** – full of ominous significance.
- Unsettling – as if they have a life of their own.

Ironic narrative

Some poems tell a story with a meaningful, and perhaps **ironic**, twist at the end. The following poem by Vanessa Kisuule tells the story of the toppling of Edward Colston's statue into Bristol Docks in 2020. Colston was involved in the slave trade but also donated to many charitable causes.

Hollow

You came down easy in the end
the righteous wrench of two ropes in a grand plie
briefly, you flew
corkscrewed, then met the ground
with the clang of toy guns, loose change
chains
a rain of cheers.

Standing ovation on the platform of your neck
punk ballet. Act 1.
there is more to come.

And who carved you?
They took such care with that stately pose and propped chin.
Wise and virtuous the plaque assured us.
Victors wish history odourless and static
but history is a sneaky mistress
moves like smoke, Colston,
like saliva in a hungry mouth.

This is your rightful home
here, in the pit of chaos with the rest of us.
Take your twisted glory and feed it to the tadpoles.
Kids will write raps to that syncopated splash.
I think of you lying in that harbour
with the horrors you hosted.
There is no poem more succinct than that.

But still
you
are permanent.
You who perfected the ratio.
Blood to sugar to money to bricks.
Each bougie building we flaunt
haunted by bones.
Children learn and titans sing
under the stubborn rust of your name.
But the air is gently throbbing with newness.

Can you feel it?

Colston, I can't get the sound of you from my head.
Countless times I passed that plinth
its heavy threat of metal and marble.
But as you landed a piece of you fell off
broke away
and inside
nothing but air.
This whole time
You were hollow.

Questions to consider

- How do sound effects, details and active verbs bring the event to life?
- At what point does the poet shift from describing the actual event?
- How does the poet reveal her attitude towards Colston?
- What point does the poet make in the twist at the end?

Summary

- Some poems use narrative to make a point.
- Not all narrative poems contain major events.
- Some poems tell a story, then explore its significance.
- Some narrative poems conclude with a meaningful twist.

Sample analysis

'Traffic' is a narrative poem in which almost nothing happens – at least to the narrator. He is stuck in traffic, the simile of him being 'stalled as if in a pit of tar' suggesting both melting tarmac on a hot day and his immobility. He begins with a realistic list of people who pass him, building up to the elderly couple, emphasising his lack of movement, but he begins to fantasise to make his point with the 'family of snails', and then the Buddha, a model of calm patience. This may suggest that the speaker is actually very frustrated, despite knowing that he should try to be like the Buddha.

Questions

QUICK TEST
1. Which of these are true statements?
   - (a) Narrative poems are always realistic.
   - (b) Some poems use narrative to make a point.
   - (c) Poets sometimes comment on their own narrative.
2. To what feature of form is narrative often linked?
3. Why does the speaker in 'Traffic' describe the things that pass him?

EXAM PRACTICE
Write one or two paragraphs explaining what you think 'A Cry from the Blue' is about, and how its narrative contributes to this.

Voice, Viewpoint, Tone and Mood

Who is speaking?

Remember that you cannot assume that the observations, memories and views in the poem are simply those of the poet. This is most obvious in poems where the poet adopts a persona, taking on the perspective of another person, real or imagined.

The poet may be trying to give readers an insight into the kind of person whose voice is presented. If so, you will need to ask yourself what this person is like, and how their outlook could be typical of a particular class of person – such as an ordinary soldier. Consider:

- their views

- how they describe themselves

- what kind of language they use.

Here is the whole of the Yeats poem introduced on page 5. It was written in 1918.

An Irish Airman Foresees his Death

I know that I shall meet my fate
Somewhere among the clouds above;
Those that I fight I do not hate,
Those that I guard I do not love;
My country is Kiltartan Cross,
My countrymen Kiltartan's poor,
No likely end could bring them loss
Or leave them happier than before.
Nor law, nor duty bade me fight,
Nor public men, nor cheering crowds,
A lonely impulse of delight
Drove to this tumult in the clouds;
I balanced all, brought all to mind,
The years to come seemed waste of breath,
A waste of breath the years behind
In balance with this life, this death.

> ## Questions to consider

- What does the airman's attitude towards death seem to be in the first two lines?
- How is this developed in the final four lines?
- Does he seem patriotic? What evidence is there?
- What people does he identify with, and how does the language emphasise this?
- What attitude to the outcome of war does he express, and how?
- What seems to be his reason for risking his life as a pilot?

Persona or metaphor?

In some poems it is obvious that a persona is being used, but it may be less obvious whether it is meant to represent a class of person, such as soldiers in general or the poor, or whether it represents an idea or a metaphor.

Read the following poem by Sheenagh Pugh once, just aiming to get a first impression of what it might be about. Begin by thinking about the title. Then read it again, considering the annotations. Try to form a picture of the imagined speaker – their desires, their moral code, and what they represent.

The Thief of Love

I will come like a thief if I have to,

soft-footed. I won't force an entry,

just find one,

some sash with a gap. I'll slip

a fingertip in, ease it open

while you're asleep.

You'll be out when I feel your cool sheets   ◄—— Very intimate. Effect?

on my skin, when I stroll through your rooms   ◄—— What is implied by this word choice?

handling, enjoying.

I'll access your email, your passwords,

click on your history, trace you

through cyberspace.

Did you think I would come to the door

| as honest folk do; play fair? | **Rhetorical question**. Effect? |

Love has no pride,

no honour; it takes what it's given

| and what it can get. It begs | Is this person a lover? A metaphor for love itself? |

without shame; why not this?

| And I am each chancer, levanter | Exotic term for someone who flees leaving unpaid debts. |

and picklock who gives his heart freely

| to what's out of reach, | The key to the persona? |

far above, safely owned, and schemes how

to coax it to hand, one way

or another.

Identifying the persona

Remember that there may not be a straightforward explanation of the poem. A poem should not be reduced to a difficult piece of detective work! How would you characterise the approach of the speaker in this poem? For example, which words below might you use?

bold	assertive	indirect	surreptitious	ethical
unscrupulous	menacing	playful	devious	stealthy

It may be that you think two or three of these words are appropriate, perhaps relating to different points in the poem. The next stage of your analysis would be to find evidence in the form of short quotations to back up your description. You should try to focus on the actual language used, not just the ideas conveyed. For example, you might say:

> The sibilance of words like 'soft', 'sash', 'slip', 'sleep', 'skin' and 'cyberspace' emphasises the stealthy, insidious invasion by this persona of someone else's private world.

Interpretations

Having worked out the character of the persona, you can consider possible interpretations. In the case of 'The Thief of Love', the title is open to interpretation too. It could refer to:

- love itself being a thief
- someone destroying love
- someone stealing a kind of intimacy – such as a stalker.

Which idea do you find more convincing, and why? What lines from the poem back up your view?

Summary

- A character through whom a poet 'speaks' a poem is called a persona.
- A persona could represent a class of person, such as a member of the Irish rural poor.
- A persona could be a metaphor.
- The persona's language is an important clue to their character and purpose.

Sample analysis

In 'The Thief of Love' the poet presents a mysterious and even sinister persona. The use of the first person and the technique of addressing the person whose privacy is invaded as 'you' creates an uncomfortable sense of intimacy, particularly in 'I feel your cool sheets / on my skin', and the sibilant 's' sounds of 'skin' and 'stroll' create a sense of this persona stealthily infiltrating someone's life, perhaps like a stalker. The mention of 'cyberspace' adds to this sound effect, but is also a real threat.

Questions

QUICK TEST

1. How does Yeats inform us about his airman's social background?
2. To whom is 'The Thief of Love' addressed, and why is this uncomfortable for the reader?
3. In which line does 'The Thief of Love' broaden the persona's identity from an individual to something more universal?

EXAM PRACTICE

Write a paragraph about the character of Yeats' airman and how the poem's details and language reveal it.

'Viewpoint' here denotes the point of view from which the poem is written. This could be:

- first person, like a 'persona poem'
- second person, addressing someone, or the reader, as 'you'
- third person, using 'he', 'she', 'it' or 'they'.

It could also be in the present or past tense. Present tense normally creates a sense of immediacy. The past tense would normally describe past events, for example the life of someone no longer living.

First-person poems

In some first-person poems, the poet is describing their own thoughts, feelings and experiences, though it is safer to write about 'the speaker', because you cannot be sure this is the case.

Contrast the persona poems in the previous section with the following poem, in which it is likely that the poet is simply expressing her own feelings:

A Birthday

My heart is like a singing bird ◄─── | Series of present-tense similes expressing joy.

    Whose nest is in a water'd shoot;

My heart is like an apple-tree

    Whose boughs are bent with thickset fruit;

My heart is like a rainbow shell

    That paddles in a halcyon sea; | **Halcyon** – idyllically tranquil, warm and happy

My heart is gladder than all these

    Because my love is come to me.

Raise me a dais of silk and down; ◄─── | Series of commands, as if she is a queen – must be how she feels.

    Hang it with vair and purple dyes; | **Vair** – squirrel fur – a luxury.

Carve it in doves and pomegranates,

    And peacocks with a hundred eyes;

Work it in gold and silver grapes,
　　In leaves and silver fleurs-de-lys;
Because the birthday of my life
　　Is come, my love is come to me.

Christina Rossetti

> **Fleurs-de-lys** – a stylised three-headed lily used in royal coats of arms.

> More than just a birthday?

> A human lover, or is this a religious poem?

Second-person poems

A first-person poem could address a lover or friend, but it is also possible for a poem to be entirely in the second person, without using the 'I' of the speaker or poet. For example, the poet may wish to commemorate someone who has died, as in the poem below.

Often the poet refers to their relationship with the person addressed, or reveals their feelings towards them, as in the beginning of Patience Agbabi's 'R.A.P. *for Carl St Hill'*.

> The last song you sang was a love song
>
> that took your whole life to write
>
> and the room crammed with home grown men
>
> cried like they were shedding blood
>
> ink on love letters
>
> as your minor chords cast their spell.

The alliteration of 'last', 'love' and 'life' links these words meaningfully and creates a mood of tender longing. The image of 'blood ink' in 'love letters' adds a sense of loss. 'Minor chords' usually sound sad. 'Spell' implies that the power of the dead man's music lives on.

Third-person poems

This is a common type of poem. You may, for example, be presented with a poem describing a character. Just as in a novel, the character could be revealed in several ways, including appearance, actions, speech and direct description.

Details

The following poem reveals character through physical details – the contents of a van:

White Van Man

He had a convenience store
on the dashboard:

a half-eaten sandwich in its box
two chocolate snack wrappers
one full fizzy drink can, one crushed
yesterday's Mirror open at the football;
sturdy gloves (large size)
rather thin on the right thumb;
aviator-style sun glasses hooked on the steering wheel
one lens cracked.

On the passenger seat:
a hard hat and hi-viz jacket
once bright yellow
draped over a grubby clipboard, biro attached.

On the floor:
a confetti of boiled sweet wrappers
obscuring a half-bottle of water
parked under the accelerator.

No Tools Are Kept In This Van Overnight
said a sticker on the rear door;
no brains either had been added in the grime.

What nobody could see until after the accident
was a fusty sleeping bag in the back
an electric razor
a dog-eared photo of his kids.

Gillian Penrose

Ask yourself

- What is implied by the opening stanza, including its tense?
- What do the details tell you about the man's lifestyle?
- What does the association of 'crushed', 'cracked', 'grubby' and 'grime' with this man imply?
- What context for this account do you imagine? Why?

Appearance, description and actions

The poem below is in the second person. The speaker describes a visit to the home of the addressed person's parents. The description conveys their character.

from 'Close Encounters III'

Inside your parents' home,

a place where the sun

could not reach nor warm,

> Implies a lack of emotional warmth.

it was arid, barren, worn.

Here 20 years had passed

with the blinds drawn.

No music ever played,

as your mother suffered

> What does the verb choice imply? (And could it be ironic?)

from constant headaches.

Shoes hugged the front door

while our slippered feet moved surreptitiously.

> What does the sibilance suggest about how the visitors feel and behave?

In this house joy was held

tight in a fist, nothing fed or nurtured

> What does this striking image suggest?

but plastic plants grew miraculously.

Dust seeped through cellophane covers,

> What does the parents' main concern seem to be?

and the cooker continued to collect grime
despite its careful, foil skin.

Raman Mundair

Summary

- Poems can be in the first, second or third person.
- A first-person poem might describe the speaker's feelings and thoughts.
- A third-person poem might convey character through the details of someone's life, appearance, likes and loves, and actions.
- Word choices may reflect character.

Sample analysis

In 'White Van Man' a sense of character is built up by physical details. The man bought his daily requirements in convenience stores. He may have been interrupted in eating his sandwich – perhaps by the accident in the final stanza. He seems to have done a largely physical job with an element of danger, shown by the hard hat, hi-viz jacket and worn gloves. The mess of wrappers implies that he only had himself to please, the 'fusty' sleeping bag that his van was his home, perhaps due to divorce. He must have viewed the 'dog-eared' photo frequently, missing his children. The words 'crushed', 'cracked', 'grubby' and 'grime' imply a broken and unloved life, the sadness of which is deepened by the man's anonymity.

Questions

QUICK TEST
1. What four pronouns denote the third person?
2. How do the two stanzas of 'A Birthday' contrast with each other?
3. What is the likely effect of a poem using the present tense?
4. How does the phrase 'where the sun could not reach nor warm' in 'Close Encounters' convey character?

EXAM PRACTICE
Write a paragraph about how details and descriptive language imply character in 'Close Encounters III'.

Tone and Mood

These terms are sometimes used loosely to mean the same thing, and sometimes they are very closely related. However, it is more accurate to define them as follows:

- tone is the manner in which the poet addresses the reader, or someone to whom the poem is directed – such as conversationally, intimately, formally or informally
- mood is the overall emotional effect of the poem – though the mood can also change as the poem develops, especially in a long poem.

Tone

Read the following poem, addressed to someone who has died. Consider the way in which the speaker addresses the person who is the subject of the poem, the kind of language used, and the way it uses repetition of the opening line.

Being Dead

For Patricia T

It doesn't really suit you, being dead.

You were the world's bright-eyed receptionist. ◄ | A literal receptionist? A receiver of the world? Both?

You held the important numbers in your head.

I never thought to view you in such a bed

Laid out in this quiet place of rest.

It doesn't quite become you, being dead. ◄ | Varies wording.

A bird's brilliance filled the life you led.

I'm glad you've kept the bangles at your wrist

As all the jingling numbers leave your head. ◄ | Sound effect, like phone ringing.

The tittle-tattle now, it must be said, ◄ | Gossip – but what kind?

Without your talent lacks its former zest. ◄ | Formal tone – used ironically?

It isn't quite your style, this being dead.

So spry you were. For counsel now instead

> Formal word for 'advice'.

We'll make enquiry at the wind's front desk.
It really doesn't suit you being dead.
You go with all our numbers round your head.

Paul Matthews

Ask yourself

- Is the poem flippant, given the subject, or just lively?
- What is the speaker's attitude to the person addressed?
- How is polite or formal language used for effect?
- How does the poet give a sense of what the person was like?
- What is the rhyme scheme, and how does it affect the tone?

Mood

Every poem has a mood, but a poem with a strong emotional content will have a more obvious mood. The poem below contains great emotional power. It could be compared with 'Being Dead' in that it is addressed to someone deceased, but as if they are still alive. Both poets, in very different ways, seem to struggle with the fact that the woman addressed is no longer alive. Read 'The Voice' aloud to get its full effect.

The Voice

Woman much missed, how you call to me, call to me,
Saying that now you are not as you were
When you had changed from the one who was all to me,

> Sounds as if something went wrong *before* she died.

But as at first, when our day was fair.

Can it be you that I hear? Let me view you, then,

> He hardly dares believe it.

Standing as when I drew near to the town
Where you would wait for me: yes, as I knew you then,
Even to the original air-blue gown!

Or is it only the breeze, in its listlessness

Travelling across the wet mead to me here, ◄——— Back to reality of wintry meadow.

You being ever dissolved to wan wistlessness, ◄——— *Wan* is pale; *wistlessness* probably means 'unknowing'.

Heard no more again far or near?

Thus I; faltering forward, ◄——— Rhythm changes – effect?

Leaves around me falling,

Wind oozing thin through the thorn from norward,

And the woman calling.

Thomas Hardy

Ask yourself

- What is the effect of the strong rhythm, and its change in the final stanza?
- The mood of this poem is never happy, but how does it change?
- How does sensory appeal affect the mood of the poem? Look especially at stanzas 2 and 4.
- How would you sum up the mood at the end, and what especially creates this?

This next poem is by a poet born in Edinburgh to a Nigerian father and Scottish mother. She was adopted by a white Scottish couple.

In My Country

walking by the waters,

down where an honest river

shakes hands with the sea,

a woman passed round me

in a slow, watchful circle,

as if I were a superstition;

or the worst dregs of her imagination,

so when she finally spoke

her words spliced into bars

of an old wheel. A segment of air.

Where do you come from?

'Here,' I said, 'Here. These parts.'

Jackie Kay

Ask yourself

- What is the effect of the personification of the river and sea?
- What is the passing woman's reaction to the speaker/poet?
- What is the emotional effect of 'worst dregs'?
- What is the poet's tone? Is it, for example, angry, disappointed, proud?

Summary

- Tone is related to the poet's style of address; mood more to emotional effect.
- Rhyme and formal language used ironically can influence tone.
- Strongly emotional poems have a more obvious mood.
- Mood can develop as a poem progresses.

Sample analysis

In 'Being Dead', the tone is surprisingly light, given the subject. The speaker addresses the deceased subject directly, using **litotes** (understatement) ironically, as if being dead were something that someone could wear, like a dress. He seems to do this to convey how alive the woman always seemed, emphasised by the onomatopoeic 'bangles' and 'jingling'. The playful and slightly mischievous 'tittle-tattle' adds the idea that the woman was very engaged in other people's lives, while the fact that it now 'lacks its former zest' is playfully formal, also suggesting her playfulness.

Questions

QUICK TEST
1. What is the difference between tone and mood?
2. What kind of poems have a more obvious mood?
3. What techniques make 'Being Dead' seem light-hearted?
4. What techniques particularly change the mood in 'The Voice'?

EXAM PRACTICE
Write a paragraph explaining how sensory details and rhythm develop the mood in 'The Voice'.

Forms

Rhythm and metre (prosody)

All poems have rhythms, but not all use a metre. A rhythm is simply a pattern created by the natural occurrence of stressed and unstressed syllables in speech – because we do not speak like robots. For example:

> I <u>put</u> my <u>hat</u> up<u>on</u> my <u>head</u>
> And <u>walked</u> in<u>to</u> the <u>Strand</u>
> And there I met another man
> Whose hat was in his hand.
>
> *Samuel Johnson*

The stressed syllables are underlined in the first two lines. Where would they come in the remaining two? Tap out the rhythm while speaking the lines aloud. Try speaking a line with the opposite emphasis: it will sound very odd:

> <u>I</u> put <u>my</u> hat u<u>pon</u> <u>my</u> head

Types of rhythm

When you write about rhythm, it is important to analyse how it helps to create the meaning and impact of the poem, and how the poet varies it for effect. Not many good poems are entirely in one rhythm. Bear in mind, too, that although it is helpful to know the technical terms in this section, so you can use them as short-hand to refer to the rhythms, the really important thing is to notice the rhythms and comment on their effects.

Iambic rhythm

The commonest rhythm is iambic. This uses a metrical foot of two syllables – an unstressed followed by a stressed. In the iambic rhythm each foot is an **iamb**.

Shakespeare wrote most of his verse in iambic rhythm, as in:

> My <u>mis</u>tress' <u>eyes</u> are <u>no</u>thing <u>like</u> the <u>sun</u>

Trochaic rhythm

A **trochee** is a foot of two syllables, one stressed and one unstressed – the opposite of an iamb. It creates a forceful, pounding rhythm, as in Henry Longfellow's 'The Song of Hiawatha', which imitates Native American drumming:

By the shore of Gitche Gumee,
By the shining Big-Sea-Water,
At the doorway of his wigwam,
In the pleasant Summer morning,
Hiawatha stood and waited.

Poems written entirely in trochees are rare, and those that employ trochaic lines normally omit the final syllable, as in John Donne's 'Song: Go and Catch a Falling Star':

Go and catch a falling star,
   Get with child a mandrake root,
Tell me where all past years are,
   Or who cleft the devil's foot,
Teach me to hear mermaids singing,
Or to keep off envy's stinging,
    And find
    What wind
Serves to advance an honest mind.

Dactylic rhythm

A dactyl is a foot of three syllables, one stressed and two unstressed. It tends to create a dragging, solemn effect, though in Tennyson's 'The Charge of the Light Brigade' it also sounds like cantering horses' hooves:

Half a league, half a league,
Half a league onward,
All in the valley of Death
   Rode the six hundred.

Anapaestic rhythm

An **anapaest** is a rhythmic foot of three syllables, two unstressed and one stressed. It creates a rolling, galloping or charging effect, as in Byron's 'The Destruction of Sennacherib'. Read the lines out loud to hear their effect:

The Assyrian came <u>down</u> like the <u>wolf</u> on the <u>fold</u>,

And his cohorts were gleaming in purple and gold

However, the anapaest is also used in comic verse, notably the **limerick**:

There <u>was</u> a young <u>man</u> from Dun<u>dee</u> ...

Metre

The metre of a poem is its rhythmic pattern, including the types and numbers of feet it has in a line. The name of a metre combines its rhythm with the number of its feet. Metre is often reinforced by rhyme, with a rhyme coming at the end of some, or all, lines. It can also be made to seem less rigid, and more natural, by the use of **enjambment** to continue the sense from one line to the next.

Pentameter

The commonest English verse form is **iambic pentameter**. Remember that an 'iamb' is a foot of one unstressed and one stressed syllable: *di-<u>dum</u>*. The prefix *pent*, from Greek, means 'five'. So, a line of iambic pentameter has five iambic feet.

The **blank verse** mostly used by Shakespeare in his plays is unrhymed (blank) iambic pentameter.

Tetrameter

Tetrameter refers to a line of four feet. Samuel Johnson's rhyme on page 32 is in **iambic tetrameter**:

I <u>put</u> / my <u>hat</u> / up<u>on</u> / my <u>head</u>

Trimeter

Trimeter refers to a line of three feet. It is more unusual, but is used in some nursery rhymes:

Cock-a /-doodle/ -do

The dame / has lost / her shoe.

Some lines in 'A Small Girl Swinging' are in trimeter:

My skirt flew off the world

These help to give the poem its childlike quality.

Traditional metres

Some traditional poetic forms employ set metres and rhyme schemes. You do not need to learn these, but it is worth knowing about one example, the **ballad**. A ballad tells a story, and most are quite long, so you are unlikely to be given one in the exam. However, you may be given a poem in **ballad metre**.

Ballad metre is in stanzas of four lines (**quatrains**). Lines 1 and 3 are in tetrameter (four feet); lines 2 and 4 are in trimeter (three feet). Lines 2 and 4 usually rhyme.

An example is Coleridge's 'The Rime of the Ancient Mariner', which tells the story of a sailor losing all his shipmates:

> Day after day, day after day,
>
> We stuck, nor breath nor motion;
>
> As idle as a painted ship
>
> Upon a painted ocean.

Summary

- Rhythm is the pattern of stressed and unstressed syllables.
- Different rhythms have different effects.
- A metre is a pattern of rhythm and number of metrical feet.
- You should comment on how rhythm creates meaning and impact.

Sample analysis

John Donne uses a powerful trochaic rhythm that sounds like a magic spell being chanted. This fits with the poem presenting a series of imperatives: 'Go ... Get ... Tell ... Teach'. The impact of each fresh command is accentuated by these monosyllabic words. He gives a list of impossible supernatural challenges. However, the point of the first stanza is that it is equally hard to avoid the effects of envy, or to find how to benefit from honesty. The metre suddenly changes, slowing the reader down to consider this. The effect is increased by the rhyming triplet at the end.

Questions

QUICK TEST
1. What is the most common rhythm in English poetry?
2. What is 'pentameter'?
3. What is a metrical 'foot'?
4. How do poets use rhythm to create or reflect their meaning?

EXAM PRACTICE
Reread 'A Small Girl Swinging' (page 12). Write a paragraph analysing how it creates meaning and character by its use of rhythm.

Structure

To comment on rhythm or language, you 'zoom in' and look at the details of a poem; to comment on structure, you have to 'zoom out' and get an overview. This is like looking at a landscape instead of at one flower!

To analyse the structure of a poem, consider:

- Does the poem tell a story?
- Does it develop ideas over the course of the poem?
- Does the mood change, or intensify?
- Does the rhythm change the pace – as in the last stanza of 'The Voice' (pages 29–30)?
- Do stanzas (see below) break the poem up into stages of development?

Stanzas

A stanza is a separate section of a poem. Sometimes the word 'verse' is used for this division, but 'stanza' avoids confusion. The previous section of this guide explained how a poetic metre repeats itself in each stanza. However, some poems that do not use a metre still use stanzas. Sometimes the stanzas reflect the structure, for example, by introducing new ideas or thematic developments.

In the following poem, stanzas relate to the metre and structure the development of the poet's ideas.

Piano

Softly, in the dusk, a woman is singing to me;
Taking me back down the vista of years, till I see
A child sitting under the piano, in the boom of the tingling strings
And pressing the small, poised feet of a mother who smiles as she sings.

In spite of myself, the insidious mastery of song
Betrays me back, till the heart of me weeps to belong
To the old Sunday evenings at home, with winter outside
And hymns in the cosy parlour, the tinkling piano our guide.

So now it is vain for the singer to burst into clamour
With the great black piano appassionato. The glamour
Of childish days is upon me, my manhood is cast
Down in the flood of remembrance, I weep like a child for the past.

D. H. Lawrence

Like many poems, this tells a story. It is in three stages:

- **Stanza 1** sets the scene. The speaker is listening to a woman singing, and it makes him remember himself as a child sitting under the piano while his mother plays and sings.
- **Stanza 2** describes how the seductive power of music ('insidious mastery of song') returns him emotionally to the 'cosy parlour' of his childhood, with his mother at the piano.
- **Stanza 3** returns to the present, saying it is pointless ('vain') for the woman to sing, accompanied by the grand piano. He is not really listening, because he is swept away by the alluring magical power ('glamour') of his memories, so that he weeps for his lost childhood.

How detail reflects structure

Now read Lawrence's poem again to see how its language fits its development.

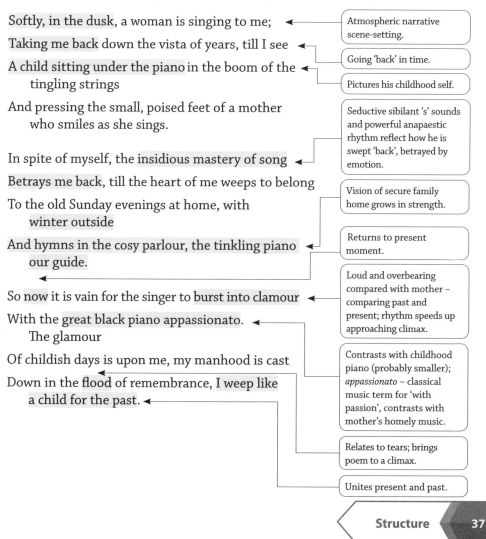

Softly, in the dusk, a woman is singing to me; ◄——— Atmospheric narrative scene-setting.

Taking me back down the vista of years, till I see ◄——— Going 'back' in time.

A child sitting under the piano in the boom of the ◄——— tingling strings — Pictures his childhood self.

And pressing the small, poised feet of a mother who smiles as she sings.

Seductive sibilant 's' sounds and powerful anapaestic rhythm reflect how he is swept 'back', betrayed by emotion.

In spite of myself, the insidious mastery of song ◄——

Betrays me back, till the heart of me weeps to belong

Vision of secure family home grows in strength.

To the old Sunday evenings at home, with winter outside

Returns to present moment.

And hymns in the cosy parlour, the tinkling piano ◄—— our guide.

Loud and overbearing compared with mother – comparing past and present; rhythm speeds up approaching climax.

So now it is vain for the singer to burst into clamour ◄——

With the great black piano appassionato. ◄—— The glamour

Contrasts with childhood piano (probably smaller); *appassionato* – classical music term for 'with passion', contrasts with mother's homely music.

Of childish days is upon me, my manhood is cast

Down in the flood of remembrance, I weep like a child for the past. ◄——

Relates to tears; brings poem to a climax.

Unites present and past.

The sonnet

Sometimes the structure is linked to a particular verse form, so look out for this in the exam.

The most obvious verse form relating to structure is the **sonnet**. Sonnets are rhyming poems of fourteen lines of iambic pentameter. In the **Petrarchan sonnet**, the first eight lines (the **octave**) put forward an idea, while the final six (the **sestet**) develop it in a new direction, often bringing it to a resolution. The **Shakespearean sonnet** has a different rhyme scheme, and usually saves the change of direction for a final rhyming **couplet**.

The sonnet below, like many sonnets, is addressed by the speaker to her beloved. In subject, it could be compared with 'Night' on page 4. It is a Shakespearean sonnet because its twist (relating to the title) comes in the final rhyming couplet.

The Trick

In a wasted time, it's only when I sleep

that all my senses come awake. In the wake

of you, let day not break. Let me keep

the scent, the weight, the bright of you, take

the countless hours and count them all night through

till that time comes when you come to the door

of dreams, carrying oranges that cast a glow

up into your face. Greedy for more

than the gift of seeing you, I lean in to taste

the colour, kiss it off your offered mouth.

For this, for this, I fall asleep in haste,

willing to fall for the trick that tells the truth

    that even your shade makes darkest absence bright,

    that shadows live wherever there is light.

Imtiaz Dharker

Ask yourself

- What is the central paradox or contradiction of the poem?
- In what ways does the poem seem dreamlike?
- What is the effect of 'you' and 'your' being used so much?
- What is the effect of the light–dark contradiction in the final couplet?

Summary

- A stanza is a paragraph in a poem. In metrical poems, the metre repeats itself in each stanza.
- Stanzas can reflect structure.
- Language and rhythm reflect structure.
- In Petrarchan sonnets, the octave sets out an idea, and the sestet develops it. A Shakespearean sonnet has a twist in a final rhyming couplet.

Sample analysis

'Piano' tells a short story that moves from present to past, and then back to the present. Stanza 1 creates an atmospheric narrative setting, with the sibilant 'Softly, in the dusk', and reveals that the poet, or speaker, is at a concert listening to a piano and vocalist. The sound takes him gradually back to his childhood as if his eyes travel over a landscape 'vista' to somewhere in the far distance. The second stanza remains largely in the past, as the 'cosy' picture of the secure family home intensifies, even though it is the present 'mastery of song' that takes him there. The final stanza shocks the reader back into the present with the word 'clamour', comparing unfavourably with the childhood memories. The poem reaches a climax in the metaphorical 'flood' of memory, concluding with the union of past and present as the speaker weeps for the past.

Questions

QUICK TEST
1. How do stanzas often relate to metre?
2. What simple and common structure does 'Piano' follow?
3. What tense is 'Piano' written in, and how might this reinforce its main theme?
4. What are the names for the two parts of a traditional sonnet?

EXAM PRACTICE
Write a paragraph analysing the effect of structure in 'The Trick'.

Language

Word choice, connotation and symbolism

Every word of a poem has been specifically chosen by the poet. You will never appreciate a poem fully or analyse it successfully if you just explore its ideas or its story, and not its language.

Tone

This guide has already explored tone in terms of the poet's way of addressing the reader. It can also be applied to individual words, especially to their level of formality. In 'A Small Girl Swinging' (page 12) the tone of 'My tummy jiggled' is childishly informal. A more formal, adult version would be 'My stomach churned', but this lacks the effect of childish naivety.

Similarly, in 'Being Dead' (pages 28–29), 'tittle-tattle' is informal and suggests slightly improper but largely harmless gossip. The word 'gossip' would lack the same hint of mischievous impropriety.

Another example of tone is found in 'Piano' (page 36). Lawrence writes: 'it is vain for the singer to burst into clamour'. 'Vain' here means 'useless' or 'pointless', but there is a hint of the more modern meaning of 'self-admiring'. This fits with the critical tone of 'burst into clamour'. To 'burst' into song sounds sudden and insensitive; worse, 'clamour' indicates a loud, annoying, attention-seeking noise, like dogs barking.

Connotations

A **connotation** is an association. We all associate different words with different things. We might, for example, associate 'snow' with cold, Christmas, purity, fun or avalanches. Poets choose words for their connotations as well as for their sound. Often, they intend more than one connotation.

Words in poems, then, frequently have layers of meaning, rather than a single straightforward one. For example, what do you associate with the word 'glamour'? You could write the word on a sheet of paper and add your ideas in a spider diagram or 'thought shower' around it.

When, in 'Piano', Lawrence writes 'The glamour / Of childish days is upon me', 'glamour' is a surprising choice. He implies that he has been overpowered. The word suggests a powerful but untrustworthy attraction. This relates to an old meaning of the word – 'enchantment'. Even now, someone might write about 'the tempting glamour of the fashion world', implying that it is less appealing beneath the glossy surface.

In Lawrence's poem, the negative connotations of 'glamour' link to the earlier lines: 'In spite of myself, the insidious mastery of song / Betrays me back ...'. 'Insidious' suggests damage that happens gradually, unnoticed, caused by cunning. 'Betrays' has even more obviously negative connotations.

We could therefore say that 'glamour' is ambiguous: it has more than one meaning. Furthermore, it expresses the speaker's mixed feelings about being overcome by possibly unreliable memories.

Symbolism

Symbolism refers to things mentioned in a poem that somehow represent broader ideas. In the two poems that follow, two modern poets write about church bell-ringing and draw out their ideas about what the activity signifies. In each poem, the same central symbol is used in different ways.

Bell-ringers (campanologists) stand in a circle and pull ropes connected to the bells in a tower above. The bell's swinging pulls the rope back up. The ringers pull in a sequence to create a repeated tune.

Bell Ringers

This is the factory floor

where all the clanging parts

are hammered, welded into one:

> Onomatopoeia; 'parts' as in bell mechanism, musical parts, and ringers?

a circle of workers lift

arms to pull down molten heaven

on their heads and thresh it

> Farmers thresh corn to get the grain.

for all it's worth in a great collapse

of scaffolding, then feel the answering

tug of grace that draws them up

> Sounds like falling scaffolding? Parts linked like scaffolding?

the living cord to a deep

well above: the engine room

of a heart that's hauling a whole

> Paradoxical image.

invisible world down to make it

matter, sending at each stroke a rush

of light into the perfect, ringing

> Pun: can mean stuff (noun) and count for something (verb).

bowl each single presence of mind

makes by being separate together.

> Ringers concentrate individually to make joint music.

Matthew Barton

Campanologists

It is as if they are milking the idea

Like cows – effect?

of angels, trying to draw down heaven

through the tower with the strain

Pun: effort and music.

they are creating, cancelling fear

of the grave's silence by railing against

a mute God via the bells' din,

God does not speak to them.

the raucous tintinnabulation

Onomatopoeia suggests loud ringing.

that airs their complaints

and grievances for over an hour

while they stand in a circle, facing

each other, wordlessly embracing

thick ropes which transmit power

to unseen clappers as twilight falls

Atmospheric contrast – suggests death?

around the church like a soft mist

completely at odds with each red fist

and the manic rhythm, the crazed pulse

of complaint and entreaty, ringing the changes

yet still getting nowhere other than bed

– that linen tomb – when all is said

Pun: at the end of the day, but also, the dead can no longer speak or act.

and done: the patterns, the exchanges.

Paul Groves

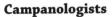

- What words in stanza 1 link to the human world?
- What metaphor describes the kingfisher in stanza 2?
- How does line 1 of stanza 3 relate to the human world?
- What are the 'spilt diamonds' in stanza 4?

Tench

The lake at dawn, a misted willow mirror.
Cast my line, shiver and wait,
the lipstick red tip of the float
an antenna to a clouded weed world.

First a flicker,
rippling like an infant's fingerprint
on a glass-topped table.
Then a plunge, rod bending, line taut.

Time stops. You break into thin air.
I reel you in:
tench, your slime-smooth skin the dark olive
of the depths you were dragged from.

Steve Eddy

Ask yourself

- What does the metaphor in line 1 describe?
- How is the fishing float (that bobs down when a fish takes the bait) 'an antenna'?
- What is the effect of the simile in stanza 2?
- How does alliteration contribute to the sense of the final line?

Summary

- Metaphors speak of something as if it *is* something else.
- Similes compare one thing with another using 'like', 'as' or 'than'.
- Personification describes an abstract idea as if it were a person or a god.
- Imagery works by comparing things that are similar in at least one way, but different in others.

Sample analysis

'Nile Kingfisher' uses a metaphor to compare the kingfisher with a jet, emphasising its power, and its direct, purposeful flight. The image of 'a short-haul scheduled flight' describes it in terms of a routine aspect of the human technological world, because the bird is just going about its daily business. The metaphor of water drops as 'spilt diamonds', however, presents the bird as a wonder of nature.

Questions

QUICK TEST
1. What kind of image uses 'like', 'as' or 'than'?
2. What is personification?
3. How does Wilfred Owen personify dawn in 'Exposure'?
4. How does 'Nile Kingfisher' use imagery to compare things from different worlds?

EXAM PRACTICE
Write a paragraph analysing the impact of imagery in 'Tench'.

Sound Effects: alliteration, assonance, onomatopoeia, repetition

Alliteration

This describes the repetition of consonant (non-vowel) sounds, especially at the beginnings of words, as in the tongue twister 'Round and round the rugged rocks the ragged rascal ran'. Here the alliteration is on the 'r' sounds at the beginnings of words, but the effect is similar if the repeated sound is at the start of a mid-word syllable:

> The alligator's grin was growing.

Remember: it is the sound that creates alliteration, not the letter. So, which of these lines includes alliteration?

- Celia came to China.

- Charlie lives in Canberra.

- Freddy's on the phone.

This is one reason why you should try to 'hear' a poem in your head even if you cannot read it aloud – for example in the exam room.

The effect of alliteration is to emphasise the alliterated words, or to increase their sound effect. For example, in 'Exposure', Wilfred Owen describes snow falling on men in World War One trenches:

> Pale flakes with fingering stealth come feeling for our faces

The repeated soft 'f' sounds suggest the soft but insistent snow.

Assonance

This refers to the repetition of vowel sounds, as in these lines from 'Exposure':

> Low drooping flares confuse our memory
>
> Watching, we hear the mad gusts tugging on the wire,
>
> Like twitching agonies of men among its brambles.

The effect is partly to bring a sense of softening harmony to something otherwise almost unbearable, but also to connect the words that have the assonance, linking their meanings.

Rhyme is based on assonance, and is used in some poems to create a sense of harmony, usually at the ends of lines, but also sometimes within lines (**internal rhyme**). Rhyme tends to link or contrast words. For example, in 'Piano' (page 36), Lawrence contrasts past and present moments by rhyming 'glamour' with 'clamour'.

Onomatopoeia

This is the use of words that sound like their meaning. For example:

jangle   boom   roar   whizz   fizz   pop   plop   flutter   crash

The effect is often to bring a line to life by directly appealing to the senses. For example, in 'Exposure', Wilfred Owen contrasts the awful bleakness of winter in the trenches with the cosiness of the remembered fireplaces at home: 'crickets jingle there'. The word 'jingle' imitates the sound of the insects, suggests music, and offers a momentary sense of relief.

Repetition

You have probably been told to avoid repetitions of words close to each other, but in poetry this can be a deliberate technique that could be called a sound effect.

Below are three poems that use some of the effects above, as well as repetition of whole words and phrases to reinforce the message of the poem.

Fall Snow

Fall snow and cover all the hurt we've done

to one another. Overlay the ache

of lovelessness with your oblivion.

You kiss me with forgiveness, make loss one

dress of silence, flake by flake:

fall snow and cover all the hurt we've done

with soft resolve. There's nothing that you shun

so kneel down from the night and cloak

our lovelessness with your oblivion.

We can't relent. And soon we will be gone.

But soothe us snow, erase our harsh mistake:

fall snow and cover all the hurt we've done

and bless us despite ourselves. Though none
but we can make amends, your whisperings speak
all lovelessness into oblivion.

Cover our traces as we stumble on:
fill up our tracks, keep tumbling full and thick –
fall snow and cover all the hurt we've done,
spread over lovelessness oblivion.

Matthew Barton

Ask yourself

- What is the effect of the soft 'f' alliteration in stanza 2, and the phrase 'soft resolve' in stanza 3, combining sibilance and assonance?
- What lines or phrases are repeated, or almost repeated, and what is the effect?
- What is the effect of internal rhyme (also assonance) in the final stanza ('stumble', 'tumbling')?
- How does the poet personify the snow, and what is the effect?

Rain

Rain, midnight rain, nothing but the wild rain
On this bleak hut, and solitude, and me
Remembering again that I shall die
And neither hear the rain nor give it thanks
For washing me cleaner than I have been
Since I was born into this solitude.
Blessed are the dead that the rain rains upon:
But here I pray that none whom once I loved
Is dying to-night or lying still awake
Solitary, listening to the rain,
Either in pain or thus in sympathy
Helpless among the living and the dead,

Like a cold water among broken reeds,

Myriads of broken reeds all still and stiff,

Like me who have no love which this wild rain

Has not dissolved except the love of death,

If love it be for what is perfect and

Cannot, the tempest tells me, disappoint.

Edward Thomas

Ask yourself
- What words are repeated, and to what effect?
- What is the effect of alliteration in 'still and stiff'?
- What is the effect of the simile 'Like a cold water among broken reeds'?
- What is the effect of the 'd' and 'p' alliteration in the final three lines?

Reggae Head

Doctors inject me

Police arrest me

Dem electric shock me

But dat nar stop me,

Oooh

Dem can't get de Reggae out me head.

Dem tek me to a station

Put me on probation,

But I still a dance

Wid de original nation,

Oooh

Dem can't get de Reggae out me head.

Benjamin Zephaniah

Ask yourself

- What is the effect of repeated verbs followed by 'me'?
- What impact does rhyme have in stanza 2?
- What is the impact of the repeated exclamation 'Ooh'?
- What is the effect of the chorus at the end of each stanza?

Summary

- Alliteration is the repetition of consonant sounds at the beginnings of words or stressed syllables.
- Assonance is the repetition of vowel sounds; it includes rhyme.
- Onomatopoeia is the use of words that sound like their meaning.
- Repetition of whole words or phrases can also be used for effect.

Sample analysis

'Fall Snow' uses alliteration and assonance to create a sense of the snow healing the emotional pain that people have caused. For example, the gentle 'l' and 'v' alliteration of 'Overlay the ache / of lovelessness with your oblivion' contrasts with the harshness of 'ache'. The harmonising effect of assonance is found in 'soft resolve', though the phrase itself is an oxymoron, expressing the need to commit to kindness. The poem also repeats lines in an almost hypnotic way, while the repetitive rhyme scheme and enjambment, as in 'done / to one another', accentuate the sense of healing.

Questions

QUICK TEST
1. Which words show alliteration in 'kneel down from the night and cloak / our lovelessness ...'?
2. What effects can alliteration have?
3. What sound effect is rhyme based on?
4. Of which sound effect are 'fizz' and 'rumble' examples?

EXAM PRACTICE
Write a paragraph analysing the use of sound and repetition in 'Rain'.

The comparison question

How the two poems will be connected

The second exam question will give you a second poem to read and ask a question like this:

> In both 'Piano' and 'Long Ago' the speakers describe childhood memories. What are the similarities and/or differences between the ways the poets present these memories?

The second poem will be more similar to the first in subject and themes than in form or style. For example, you could be given two poems about childhood memories, but not two sonnets on unrelated subjects.

Focusing on the question

The focus of the two separate questions will probably overlap. For example, if the first poem was 'A Small Girl Swinging' (page 12), the first question might be:

> In 'A Small Girl Swinging', how does the poet present childhood experiences?

If the second poem was 'Piano' (page 36), the comparison question might be:

> In both 'A Small Girl Swinging' and 'Piano' the speakers describe views of childhood. What are the similarities and/or differences between the ways the poets present these views?

Despite the overlap, it is important to focus on the exact question. Do not just compare random features. Be concise too: there are only 8 marks for this question.

'The ways the poets present …'

The all-important phrase is 'the ways the poets present …'. This refers to the aspects of voice, form and language summarised in the first section of this guide. You will not get many marks for this question without analysing techniques. So, which of the partial responses below do you think is better?

> ### Response 1
> 'A Small Girl Swinging' describes childhood as a time of fear and insecurity, though mixed with some excitement. It also comments on the child's need for the absent mother. 'Piano', on the other hand, presents childhood as a time of happiness and security, with the child's intimate relationship with the mother in the family home.

Prepare to compare

Read both unseen poems and both questions before beginning to answer the question about the first poem. This will give you a perspective on the first poem and will also allow you to notice features in the first poem that will be relevant in the second question.

As the comparison question carries only 8 marks, plan to spend about 12 minutes on it. Prepare by adding any additional annotations to the first poem that will help you to answer the question. It may be helpful to circle or colour-code the relevant annotations you have already made. Then annotate features to compare in the second poem. Aim to compare four or five similarities and differences – though you could note more and then choose.

Annotation for comparison

Reread 'Piano', and then read the new poem, 'Long Ago', which has similar themes. Both have been annotated for the following exam question:

> In both 'Piano' and 'Long Ago' the speakers describe the effects of memory. What are the similarities and/or differences between the ways the poets present this theme?

Piano

Softly, in the dusk, a woman is singing to me;

Taking me back down the vista of years, till I see ◀— | Present tense; steady rhythm of memory dragging him.

A child sitting under the piano, in the boom of ◀— | Pictures himself in detached way.
    the tingling strings

And pressing the small, poised feet of a mother
    who smiles as she sings.

In spite of myself, the insidious mastery of song

Betrays me back, till the heart of me weeps ◀— | Mixed feelings – as if memory tricks him.
    to belong

To the old Sunday evenings at home, with winter
    outside

And hymns in the cosy parlour, the tinkling piano ◄─ Nostalgic, homely language.
    our guide.

So now it is vain for the singer to burst
    into clamour
With the great black piano appassionato.
    The glamour
Of childish days is upon me, my manhood is cast ◄─ Attraction – but false?
Down in the flood of remembrance, I weep like ◄─ Climax: swept away.
    a child for the past.

Long Ago

In a house I visited when I was young
I looked in through a partly opened door. ◄─ Image of partial nature of memory.
An old man sang 'Long Ago and Far Away'
To a rocking-horse, a friend's grandfather ◄─ Sad detail – lost son's toy.
Whose first-born son was lost at sea
Half-a-century before
In a ship whose name I have forgotten.

Whenever that sad song is played or sung ◄─ Power of music.
I'm in that house again, by that same door.
A woman tugs my sleeve. 'Come away,' ◄─ Woman's anonymity; 'tugs', like memory.
She says. 'Leave him alone.'
He sings, but he's no longer there.
The rocking-horse is rocking like the sea. ◄─ Moving, haunting simile.
Ocean is everywhere
And the room is wind and rain. ◄─ Emotion linked to water.

Douglas Dunn

Ask yourself how both poems

- use the senses
- use symbolic objects
- describe the power of music
- use tenses
- use water metaphorically.

Summary

- The second poem will be similar in subject and/or theme to the first.
- Focus on the exact question.
- 'The ways the poets present ...' refers to methods.
- Spend about 12 minutes on the comparison.

Sample analysis

In both poems, music triggers emotionally evocative memories. In 'Piano', the past is seen visually as a returning 'vista', the steady rhythm reflecting its unfolding. In the detached picture of 'a child', the third-person phrasing shows the speaker's loss of his childhood self. In 'Long Ago', there is more emphasis on the loss of the child who owned the rocking horse, which, like both pianos in 'Piano', symbolises loss. Both poems, however, use images of water for emotion: the 'flood' of remembrance in 'Piano' and the ocean-filled room in 'Long Ago'.

Questions

QUICK TEST
1. What does 'the ways the poets present ...' refer to?
2. What should you focus on in answering the comparison question?
3. What key features do 'Piano' and 'Long Ago' share?
4. What is the key difference in the focus of the two poems?

EXAM PRACTICE
Write a plan for a comparison of how 'A Small Girl Swinging' and 'Long Ago' present memories of the past and their emotional effect.

Writing a Comparison

There are two main methods of comparison, differing in how they approach similarities and differences. With either method you need to ensure that you write about both poems.

For example, look again at the question used in the previous section:

> In both 'Piano' and 'Long Ago' the speakers describe the effects of memory. What are the similarities and/or differences between the ways the poets present this theme?

Despite the question typically using the phrase 'and/or differences', it is highly likely that there will be similarities *and* differences. The question will probably point out a basic similarity, so you might begin by extending this. For the question above, you could begin by writing:

In both poems, music unlocks memories in the speaker that have powerful emotional effects.

Which method to use?

You could get full marks using either method, but your comparison may be more fluent if you use the second one. On the other hand, the first is simpler. Try both and see which works better for you.

Comparison method 1

For this method, assuming you can find both similarities and differences, you write one or more paragraphs about the similarities, then one or more paragraphs about the differences. You would need to make it clear at which point you were switching. You might, for example, begin a new paragraph with one of these phrases:

- 'On the other hand, …'
- 'Despite these similarities, …'
- 'Having said that, …
- 'There are, however, significant differences …'.

Ideally, you should finish with a further short paragraph summing up your comparison. Try not to simply repeat the earlier paragraphs.

Comparison method 2

This method involves comparing one or more aspects of both poems within a paragraph, then moving on to one or more different aspects of both poems in the next paragraph. Here is a plan for the question on 'Piano' and 'Long Ago' in the previous section:

1. **Similar:** music evokes memory and returns speaker to pictured childhood scene; also in sensory nature of memory and language: in 'Piano', visual metaphor 'vista', onomatopoeia of 'tingling' and 'tinkling', touch of mother's feet; in 'Long Ago', sensation in 'tugs my sleeve'. **Different:** 'Long Ago' focuses more on sight ('partly opened door'), rocking-horse, touch ('tugs') and woman's voice; music is evocative, but is not explored in itself as in 'Piano'.

2. **Similar:** memory evokes emotion. **Different:** Lawrence explicit about feelings ('my manhood is cast down ...'). Dunn implies he is haunted by memory: 'He sings, but he's no longer there.'

3. **Similar:** strong water imagery: 'Piano' has 'flood of remembrance'; 'Long Ago' rocking-horse still 'rocking like the sea', and 'Ocean is everywhere'. **Different:** 'Piano' more about speaker's personal loss; 'Long Ago' more about dead son, and general sadness of loss.

The language of comparison

Using method 1, you definitely need to use **link words** or phrases, with the correct punctuation, when you switch from similarities to differences. For method 2, however, it is helpful to use these whenever you make a comparison. Some additional link words and phrases are:

* whereas
* however
* moreover
* by contrast/comparison
* although.

Here is the first point in the plan above expanded, using links words and phrases (underlined):

> The poems are <u>similar in that, in both,</u> music evokes memories that return the speaker to a pictured moment in childhood. <u>In addition,</u> the language of both expresses the sensory nature of memory. <u>However,</u> they use the senses in different ways. In 'Piano', 'vista' is visual, <u>but</u> the main focus is on sound, with the onomatopoeia of 'tingling' and 'tinkling', <u>whereas</u> 'Long Ago' focuses on the partial nature of memory, with the rocking-horse glimpsed through a 'partly opened door', on touch ('tugs') and the woman's words. <u>Moreover, while</u> 'Piano' gives a strong sense of both pieces of piano music, 'Long Ago' <u>merely</u> refers to the 'sad song'.

Comparing different aspects

Comparing narrative and structure

Ask yourself:

- Does each poem tell a story?
- If so, is it the story of an event?
- Does the story make a point?
- Does the structure follow the narrative?

For example, comparing 'Piano' and 'Long Ago', you could write:

'Piano' is in the present tense, and begins in the present moment, in which the speaker is listening to a concert that makes him remember himself as a child listening to his mother play piano. By contrast, 'Long Ago' starts in the past tense and initially focuses on the past, its first stanza describing a moment when the speaker saw and heard an old man singing to a rocking-horse. In stanza 2 the poem shifts time frame, explaining how the song always takes him back to that moment. However, both poems end with similarly emotional imagery, 'Piano' with the speaker carried on the 'flood' of memory, and 'Long Ago' with the speaker haunted by the horse 'rocking like the sea'.

Comparing voice, viewpoint, tone and mood

Ask yourself:

- Is each poem in the first, second or third person?
- Is it written from a particular perspective (e.g. a persona)?
- What is the tone – for example, conversational, passionate?
- What mood is created?

For 'Piano' and 'Long Ago', you could write:

'Piano' is in the first person, the speaker frankly confessing the emotional effect of a concert on him, although he describes himself as 'a child', showing his detachment from that state. 'Long Ago' is also first person, but is far more conversational in tone. Whereas in 'Piano' the speaker nostalgically describes the 'cosy parlour' of his childhood and confesses to weeping 'like a child for the past', the language of 'Long Ago' is understated, as in 'a ship whose name I have forgotten'. In 'Piano' the emotion is explicit; in 'Long Ago' it is quietly implied in the sea imagery of the last two lines.

Comparing form

Ask yourself:

* Does each poem have a metre or rhyme scheme?
* If so, what is the effect?
* How is each poem divided into stanzas?

You could write:

> *The powerful emotional experience of 'Piano' is contained by the regular aabb rhyme scheme and the lines of roughly equal length. In addition, it is structured by stanzas, the first describing the memory being evoked, the second describing how the music 'betrays' the speaker emotionally, and the third dismissing the 'clamour' of the concert. Stanza division also features in 'Long Ago'. Stanza 1 describes a childhood moment in a matter-of-fact way, while stanza 2 describes how the song always returns the speaker to that moment. It has no third stanza, but the final two lines bring an emotional climax through water imagery, though in a quieter way than in 'Piano'.*

Comparing language

Ask yourself:

* Can you compare word choices?
* What is the effect of any imagery?
* Are there noticeable sound effects, such as alliteration?

You could write:

> *'Piano' is dominated by sound, both in what it describes and how it does it. The vocalist sings 'softly in the dusk', the sibilance creating atmosphere. Lawrence uses onomatopoeia in 'boom of the tingling strings', and alliteration to suggest emotion creeping up on the listener in 'insidious mastery of song'. **Plosive** syllables burst dramatically in 'great black piano appassionato'. 'Long Ago' is much less dramatic, its iambic pentameter closer to ordinary speech, as in 'I'm in that house again, by that same door'. However, its repetition of 'rocking' in the second stanza, in another iambic line, creates a sense of waves on which the ghostly rocking-horse rocks.*

Summary

- Choose whether to write about similarities first, then differences, or to write about them both within one paragraph at a time on each aspect.
- Use linking words and phrases to signpost points of comparison.
- Compare narrative, structure and form.
- Compare word choices and language.

Sample analysis

Imagery is used in a restrained way in both poems. In 'Piano' the poet sees the past as a landscape – a 'vista' – and implies a personification of song in its 'insidious mastery' of his emotions, but its main image is the metaphorical 'flood of remembrance'. 'Long Ago' is dominated by the symbol of the dead son's rocking-horse, which rocks 'like the sea' in which he was lost. Both poems reach their climax in imagery relating water to emotion.

Questions

QUICK TEST
1. Which method of comparison is more likely to help you compare fluently?
2. What is the purpose of link words and phrases?
3. How do the stanzas relate to structure in 'Long Ago'?
4. How do 'Piano' and 'Long Ago' differ in their use of tense?

EXAM PRACTICE
Write a paragraph comparing the use of visual details in 'Piano' and 'Long Ago'.

You must be able to: understand how to approach the exam questions and meet the requirements of the mark scheme.

Quick tips

* Read both poems and questions to get an overview of your tasks and a perspective on each poem. Then reread the first poem and annotate it for answering the first question.

* Read the question carefully. It will ask you to comment on an aspect of the poem, not just to analyse the whole poem.

* Think about how to interpret the question. For example, if the first poem was 'Long Ago' (page 56), and the question was 'How does the poet present memory?', you could include how the poem presents both the operation of memory and its effects.

* The two unseen poetry questions combined carry one-third of the marks for Paper 2. So, spend about 45 minutes on them – about 33 minutes on the first poem, and 12 minutes on the comparison. Or think in terms of 30 minutes, 10 minutes, and 5 minutes to check.

* Don't just identify poetic techniques: write about their *effects*.

* Reread the question occasionally to keep yourself focused.

* Write concisely, using brief quotations to support your points.

* Focus on key details. Do not just summarise or generalise: it is better to say 'a lot about a little' rather than 'a little about a lot'.

* Bear in mind the Assessment Objectives below.

Assessment Objectives

First poem

AO1: Understand and respond to the poem (12 marks)

You should make a range of points in response to the question and the poem, supporting them with brief quotations or references, organising them logically, and writing in an appropriately formal style.

Lower	Middle	Upper
A relevant response with some explanation and some supporting references from the poem.	A clear, explained response to the question; effective use of references to support explanation.	A critical, exploratory response to the question and the poem; well-chosen, precise references to support interpretation(s).

AO2: Analyse effects of language, form and structure (12 marks)

You must analyse how word choices, language techniques, form and structure create meaning, using appropriate literary terminology (e.g. 'simile').

Lower	Middle	Upper
Identification of some poetic methods, with some comment on their effects, using some terminology.	A clear explanation of a range of poetic methods and their effects, using accurate terminology.	Insightful analysis of poetic methods and exploration of their effects, with a range of well-chosen and accurate terminology.

Comparison question

This question does not assess AO1. AO2 is assessed as for the main question, except that you will need to make comparisons and will not be expected to go into so much detail.

Lower	Middle	Upper
Some links between poets' use of language, structure or form and their effects on the reader.	A thoughtful comparison of poets' use of language, and/or structure, and/or form, and their effects; terminology used effectively to support analysis.	An exploratory and convincing comparison of poets' use of language, structure and form, and their effects; well-chosen terminology used effectively.

Read the two annotated poems below, and then the question on the first poem and annotated Grade 5 response.

Night Ferry

And our idea of hell is the night ferry.
A deep slow swell, the purser in his booth,
A thumping head no aspirin can soothe
And two or three lads quietly getting merry.

It's normal, that is all, the bottom line
Of nightmare, meaning nothing, emptiness
Which finds us though we leave it no address
And leaves a pain that art cannot refine.

It's almost three o'clock. The vessel rolls:
We draw our coats about us. The idea
Of sea enters our minds and washes clear
The bodies by their sinks and toilet bowls.

George Szirtes

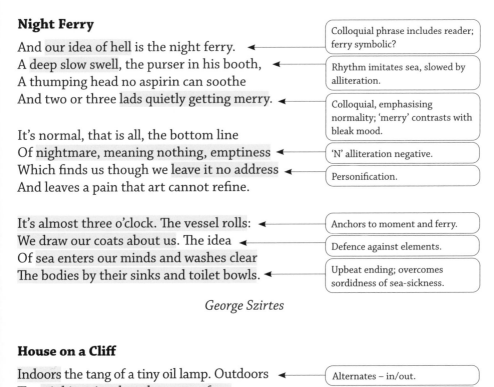

Colloquial phrase includes reader; ferry symbolic?

Rhythm imitates sea, slowed by alliteration.

Colloquial, emphasising normality; 'merry' contrasts with bleak mood.

'N' alliteration negative.

Personification.

Anchors to moment and ferry.

Defence against elements.

Upbeat ending; overcomes sordidness of sea-sickness.

House on a Cliff

Indoors the tang of a tiny oil lamp. Outdoors
The winking signal on the waste of sea.
Indoors the sound of the wind. Outdoors the
    wind.
Indoors the locked heart and the lost key.

Outdoors the chill, the void, the siren. Indoors
The strong man pained to find his red blood cools,

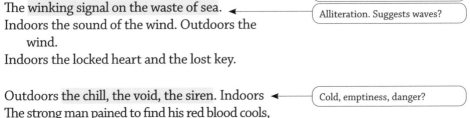

Alternates – in/out.

Alliteration. Suggests waves?

Cold, emptiness, danger?

While the blind clock grows louder, faster.
    Outdoors

Significance of time.

The silent moon, the garrulous tides she rules.

Opposites; night-time.

Indoors ancestral curse-cum-blessing. Outdoors
The empty bowl of heaven, the empty deep.

Night; metaphor emptiness.

Indoors a purposeful man who talks at cross
Purposes, to himself, in a broken sleep.

Louis MacNeice

In 'Night Ferry', how does the poet present the experience of the ferry crossing? [24 marks]

The speaker describes the ferry crossing as mostly horrible ('hell'). This is partly because of the effects of the sea.[1] There is a 'deep slow swell', which gives a feeling of the deep sea slowly rolling, and this gives the speaker 'a thumping head' that cannot be cured by aspirin, and makes other passengers throw up into 'sinks and toilet bowls'.[2] However, the purser seems to be all right, because he is in a booth, like the 'lads quietly getting merry'. This means they are able to get through the gloomy night by getting drunk at the bar. The word 'merry', which is happy, cheerful and informal, contrasts with the hell that the speaker feels.[3]

In the second verse the poet explores what the experience of the ferry crossing means, or why it is so awful. He uses quite ordinary language, 'It's normal, that is all', to say how ordinary the experience is, even though it is a 'nightmare'.[4] This seems to show a pessimistic view, as if life is a 'nightmare, meaning nothing, emptiness'. Perhaps being on the ferry in the middle of the night makes him feel negative about everything.[5]

1. Simple but effective comment on what poem is about, focusing on the question. AO1

2. Shows basic understanding, but too little analysis of words, and style sometimes too informal ('throw up'). AO1, AO2

3. Thoughtful analysis of effect of poet's word choice. AO2

4. Some attempt to analyse language. AO2

5. Attempts interpretation, but needs more evidence. AO2

The poet uses personification in the second verse. Emptiness is like a letter, or a postal worker, that finds the speaker even though he has left 'no address'. This makes it sound like this feeling of 'emptiness' cannot be avoided. It will get you even on a ferry at sea, when you are not at home.[6]

6. Accurate use of term, with thoughtful analysis – though 'it will get you' is too informal. AO2

The final verse switches to telling a sort of story. It brings the reader into the present moment by telling us the time in a short, simple sentence.[7] The ship rolling at that particular moment also gives a clear sense of the time, making us feel as if we were there.[8] The poet also appeals to the senses in 'We draw our coats about us.' This makes it clear that it is cold – he must be outside on the deck looking out at the sea. The use of the pronoun 'us' includes the reader, though maybe he is with a friend.[9]

7. Hints at narrative and begins to comment on effect of sentence form. AO2

8. Basic but effective comment on effect. AO2

9. Explores meaning, using technical term. AO2

The final sentence gives a twist.[10] At first it seems like the idea of sea is making people throw up, but maybe it is more that thinking about the sea out there actually stops him thinking about all that. In this way, the poem has a kind of happy ending, despite the experience being generally unpleasant.[11]

10. Effective topic sentence. AO1

11. Explores meaning, providing competent conclusion that refers back to question. AO1, AO2

Questions

EXAM PRACTICE

Choose one or two paragraphs from this essay. Read them through a few times, then rewrite and improve them. You could:

- Change wording and sentence types to make the style more fluent and sophisticated.
- Use better quotations and ensure that they are embedded in sentences.
- Provide a more detailed or more insightful analysis.
- Use more subject terminology.

In 'Night Ferry', how does the poet present the experience of the ferry crossing? [24 marks]

The poem describes a grim night ferry crossing that must be endured until the ferry docks. Its rhyme scheme and iambic pentameter give the experience form and make it bearable. The three stanzas structure it into a description of the crossing, an exploration of its meaning, and a final epiphany.[1]

1. Effective introduction commenting on form and structure. AO1, AO2

The opening 'And', is unsettling as if it is a continuation. The use of 'our' also creates uncertainty: it could refer to the speaker and a companion, or people generally, including the reader. 'Our idea of hell' is a colloquial exaggeration but it could also be taken literally, as if the crossing is a metaphor for hell.[2]

2. Close, insightful focus on effects of language choices. AO2

After the opening statement, the speaker justifies it. The dragging non-iambic rhythm of 'deep slow swell' combines with alliteration to create an unsettling sense of the rolling sea causing the speaker's headache, described as 'thumping', as if the sufferer is repeatedly hit, and possibly echoing the engine noise.[3] It also makes other passengers sick into 'sinks and toilet bowls'. Even 'lads quietly getting merry' at the bar is bleak. The colloquial language makes it sound commonplace, and 'merry' seems weak when contrasted with the 'hell' they are trying to keep at bay.[4] There being only 'two or three' of them also paints a sad picture. The only other passengers mentioned are just sea-sick 'bodies'.

3. Insightful analysis of language; judicious use of terminology. AO2

4. Precise analysis of word choice. AO2

In stanza 2, banal language expresses the ordinariness of the experience: 'It's normal, that is all'. It is as if the 'bottom line' of human existence is a 'nightmare'. The alliteration of 'normal', 'nightmare' and 'nothing' links these words in negativity.[5] 'Emptiness' is personified as the deliverer of an unwanted parcel that reaches us even with no address, implying that this feeling is unavoidable.[6] Even the poet's own 'art' cannot improve it.

> 5. Effective interpretation of word choice, with terminology. AO2

> 6. Insightful and fluent analysis of correctly named technique. AO2

Stanza 3 switches to a narrative, the short simple sentence announcing the time taking us into the poem's present moment, and emphasising how time drags on the crossing.[7] 'The vessel rolls' also brings the physical experience to life, aided by the sense of cold in 'draw our coats about us': passengers are doing their best to find comfort.[8] It also places the speaker on deck, along with 'us'.

> 7. Awareness of structure and use of sentence types. AO2

> 8. Insightful interpretation. AO2

In the final sentence, however,[9] the inspirational 'idea of sea' replaces the sordid discomfort of sea-sickness. It is as if the speaker has been seized by the sea's physical presence, and this has lifted 'us' out of the 'nightmare' of 'emptiness' explored in stanza 2.[10]

> 9. Effective use of link word. AO1

> 10. Insightful interpretation, supported by well-chosen embedded quotations. AO1, AO2

The poem takes an experience that has to be endured, and that is a metaphor for human suffering, and finally transcends it through a direct experience of nature.[11]

> 11. Effective conclusion summing up poem's impact without repetition. AO1, AO2

Questions

EXAM PRACTICE
Cover up the annotations, then reread the essay and try to list five of its most effective features. You could write notes on the actual essay – in pencil if you prefer.

Grade 5 Comparison

Both 'Night Ferry' and 'House on a Cliff' show human beings in a state of struggle, influenced by the elements. What are the similarities and/or differences between the ways the poets describe their feelings? [8 marks]

Both poems are about individuals at night influenced by the sea, struggling with their feelings.[1] 'Night Ferry' is clearer. The speaker hates the ferry crossing and it makes him feel empty. In 'House on a Cliff' there is a similar sense of bleakness, but no clear cause. The 'tiny oil lamp' creates a gloomy picture, with the 'waste of sea', the wind, and the man's 'locked heart'. Like the speaker of 'Night Ferry', he is unhappy ('pained'), but we don't know why, and there is less sense of his identity.[2]

In both poems it is cold. In 'Night Ferry' we know this from people drawing their coats around them, but 'House on a Cliff' is more straightforward: 'chill'. In 'Night Ferry' the 'nothing, emptiness' is the speaker's response to the crossing. In 'House on a Cliff' it is the emptiness of the night outside the house, and beyond the cliff, as well as the 'empty bowl' of the sky.[3]

Each poem is three verses, but they are structured differently. 'Night Ferry' moves from description, to discussion, to now, on deck. 'House on a Cliff', on the other hand, switches between indoors and outdoors throughout.[4] 'Night Ferry' contrasts the indoors of the bar, and the booth, and the outdoors of the deck, but it seems more natural. In 'House on a Cliff' the contrast is more dramatic and artificial.[5]

1. Effective introductory sentence.

2. Good comparative points, but explanation and evidence needed.

3. Clear comparison, though could explore imagery.

4. Effective comparison of form.

5. Interesting point but needs explanation and evidence.

There are other opposites all through 'House on a Cliff', like 'silent moon, the garrulous [talkative] tides' and 'curse' versus 'blessing'. Both poems use personification, 'Night Ferry' for the emptiness, and 'House on a Cliff' for the moon. In both cases this gives an image of power.[6]

6. Simple but effective analysis of technique's effect, using technical term.

Questions

EXAM PRACTICE

Choose one or two paragraphs from this essay. Read them through a few times, then rewrite and improve them. You could:

- Change wording and sentence types to make the style more fluent.
- Use link words to add fluency.
- Provide a more insightful analysis.
- Use more subject terminology.

Grade 7+ Comparison

Both 'Night Ferry' and 'House on a Cliff' show human beings in a state of struggle, influenced by the elements. What are the similarities and/or differences between the ways the poets describe their feelings? [8 marks]

Both poems depict individuals at night influenced by the elements, struggling with negative feelings. However, in 'Night Ferry', a narrator tries to explain why the crossing is difficult, universalising it with the pronoun 'us'. 'House on a Cliff' conveys a similar bleakness, but the reader is given a series of impressions formulaically introduced only by the alternating 'Indoors' and 'Outdoors'.[1]

1. Highly effective introduction to key similarities and differences.

Both characters are unhappy, but in 'Night Ferry' this is 'normal', whereas in 'House on a Cliff' the man's 'locked heart' suggests that he cannot love. In addition, in 'Night Ferry' the speaker's experience 'leaves a pain', whereas in 'House on a Cliff' the man is also 'pained' but more enigmatic.[2] Even the personified moon and talkative tides make him seem more isolated.[3]

2. Excellent comparison of similar language and its effects.

3. Very effective analysis of technique, using correct term.

In 'Night Ferry' passengers are joined in a shared seeking of comfort, in the bar and on deck. In 'House on a Cliff', by contrast, the man is alone, surrounded by 'the chill, the void, the siren'. All are comfortless, and the siren suggests danger.[4]

4. Insightful comparison and interpretation.

Structurally,[5] 'Night Ferry' moves from description, to exploration, to present moment narrative, while 'House on a Cliff' alternates between indoors and outdoors throughout.

5. Good use of adverb to flag up what paragraph is about.

'Night Ferry' compares indoors and on-deck, but this flows as part of the narrative. 'House on a Cliff' dramatically juxtaposes the two worlds, beginning and ending indoors.[6] This gives a sense of the man being stuck, whereas the speaker in 'Night Ferry' is finally relieved by the thought of the sea.[7]

> 6. Effective and succinct observation.

> 7. Insightful interpretation.

The narrative of 'Night Ferry' is reflected in its conversational language, its only image being the personification in stanza 2. 'House on a Cliff' is self-consciously poetic: alliteration and assonance strengthen the metaphor of the 'locked heart and the lost key', and the 'empty bowl' metaphor suggests an emotional starvation linked to the man's isolation.[8]

> 8. Excellent comparison of language, using appropriate terminology.

Questions

EXAM PRACTICE

Reread the Grade 5 and Grade 7+ comparison responses. Then write an examiner-style paragraph summarising why the Grade 7+ deserves the higher grade. Try to include four points, with examples where possible.

Consider:

- organisation
- fluency, including use of link words and phrases to signpost comparison
- level of analysis
- use of subject terminology.

1. In 'She Dwelt among the Untrodden Ways' (page 10), how does the poet present his feelings about the girl?

2. In both 'She Dwelt among the Untrodden Ways' and 'A Small Girl Swinging' (page 12) the speakers describe views of childhood. What are the similarities and/or differences between the ways the poets present these views?

3. In 'Traffic' (page 14), how does the poet present his feelings about his situation?

4. In both 'Traffic' and 'A Cry from the Blue' (pages 15–16) the speakers describe experiences of time. What are the similarities and/or differences between the ways the poets present their experiences?

5. In both 'Traffic' and 'Night Ferry' (page 65) the speakers describe difficult journeys. What are the similarities and/or differences between the ways the poets present their experiences?

6. In 'The Thief of Love' (pages 20–21), how does the poet present love?

7. The speakers of both 'The Thief of Love' and 'Fall Snow' (pages 50–51) describe aspects of love. What are the similarities and/or differences between the ways the poets present attitudes to love?

8. In 'A Birthday' (pages 23–24), how does the poet present love?

9. In both 'A Birthday' and 'Fall Snow' the speakers describe aspects of love. What are the similarities and/or differences between the ways the poets present their feelings?

10. In 'White Van Man' (page 25), how does the poet present the character and life of the man?

11. Both 'White Van Man' and 'An Irish Airman Foresees his Death' (page 19) present characters. What are the similarities and/or differences between the ways the poets present these characters?

12. In 'Being Dead' (pages 28–29), how does the poet present the character of the woman?

13. Both 'Being Dead' and 'White Van Man' present characters. What are the similarities and/or differences between the ways the poets do this?

14. In 'The Voice' (pages 29–30), the poet presents memories of a loved one. How does he present these memories and the feelings they arouse?

15. 'The Voice' and 'Piano' (page 36) both present memories. What are the similarities and/or differences between the ways the poets present memories and feelings?

16. In 'The Trick' (page 38), the poet presents an experience of love. How does she do this?

17. Both 'The Trick' and 'A Birthday' present joyful experiences. What are the similarities and/or differences between the ways the poets present these experiences?

18. Both 'The Trick' and 'Night' (page 4) are love poems. What are the similarities and/or differences between the ways the poets present love?

19. In 'Bell Ringers' (page 41), how does the poet present the experience of bell-ringing?

20. Both 'Bell Ringers' and 'Campanologists' (page 42) describe bell-ringing. What are the similarities and/or differences between the ways the poets present their views of this activity?

21. In 'Fall Snow', how does the poet present the experience of snow?

22. Both 'Fall Snow' and 'Rain' (pages 51–52) describe weather. What are the similarities and/or differences between the ways the poets present their responses to weather?

Glossary

Alliteration – repetition of consonant (non-vowel) sounds at the beginnings of words or stressed syllables (e.g. 'carving a career, making his mark').

Ambiguity (adj. 'ambiguous') – a double meaning.

Anapaest – a rhythmic foot of three syllables, two unstressed and one stressed.

Assonance – repetition of vowel sounds (e.g. fish, bit).

Ballad – narrative poem, often with a tragic ending, written in ballad metre.

Ballad metre – verse form consisting of stanzas of four lines each, in which lines 1 and 3 are in tetrameter (four feet), and lines 2 and 4 in trimeter (three feet). Lines 2 and 4 usually rhyme.

Blank verse – unrhymed (blank) iambic pentameter.

Connotation – association of a word with other things or ideas, e.g. fire with heat or passion.

Couplet – pair of lines, often rhyming.

Dactyl – a rhythmic foot of three syllables, one stressed and two unstressed.

Elegy – poem celebrating the life of someone who has died.

Enjambment – running the sense of a phrase on from one line to the next.

Epitaph – tribute to someone who has died, sometimes in verse form.

Foot – syllabic unit of rhythm, repeated to form a metre.

Form – a poem's verse patterns and how it is divided into **stanzas**.

Iamb (adj. iambic) – a verse **foot** of one unstressed syllable followed by one stressed.

Iambic pentameter – metrical line of five iambs.

Iambic tetrameter – metrical line of four iambs.

Imagery – words used to create a picture in the imagination.

Internal rhyme – rhyme within lines of verse rather than at their ends.

Irony – something seemingly inappropriate in a grimly comic way; the technique of deliberately appearing to mean one thing while actually meaning something else that contradicts it.

Limerick – comic poem of five anapaestic lines rhyming *aabba*.

Link words (connectives) – words or phrases signposting argument, such as 'however' or 'on the other hand'.

Litotes – understatement.

Metaphor – image describing something as if it *is* something else.

Metre – poem's rhythmic pattern, including the types and numbers of feet it has in a line.

Mood – overall emotional effect of a poem or a significant part of it.

Narrative (noun and adj.) – telling a story.

Octave – first eight lines of a Petrarchan sonnet, which put forward an idea.

Onomatopoeia – use of words that sound like their meaning, e.g. 'fizz'.

Oxymoron – combination of apparently contradictory ideas, e.g. 'cold fire'.

Pentameter – line of verse with five feet, especially iambic pentameter.

Persona – narrator or speaker of a poem assuming a particular identity, e.g. 'An Irish Airman Foresees his Death'.

Personification – type of metaphor describing an abstract idea, such as love or time, as if it were a person or a god.

Petrarchan sonnet – a poem of 14 lines, in which the first eight (the octave) put forward an idea, while the final six (the sestet) develop it in a new direction, often bringing it to a resolution.

Plosive – consonant speech sound that seems to explode, created by sudden release of air, e.g. in 'black piano appassionato'.

Pun – play on a word with two meanings, e.g. 'strain' meaning both effort and tune.

Quatrain – four-line stanza.

Rhetorical question – question asked for effect rather than expecting an answer.

Rhyme – sound effect produced by a repeated vowel sound and consonant, but with a different consonant sound following it.

Rhyme scheme – pattern of rhyme; can be denoted by letters, as in *abab*.

Semantic field – broad grouping of words associated with a particular area of life, e.g. science.

Sestet – six lines ending a Petrarchan sonnet.

Shakespearean sonnet – 14-line poem with a twist or resolution in a final rhyming couplet.

Sibilance (adj. sibilant) – use of hissing sounds, especially 's', but also 'sh'.

Simile – image comparing one thing with another explicitly, using 'like', 'as' or 'than'.

Sonnet – 14-line poem; *see also* **Petrarchan sonnet; Shakespearean sonnet.**

Stanza – separate section within a poem.

Symbol – an object used to represent an idea.

Symbolism – using an object or colour to represent a specific idea or meaning.

Tetrameter – line of four metrical feet.

Theme – idea explored in a poem, beyond its obvious subject, e.g. childhood innocence.

Tone – how the poet addresses the reader – for example, in a conversational tone, or a bitter tone.

Trimeter – line of three metrical feet.

Trochee (adj. trochaic) – metrical foot of two syllables, one stressed and one unstressed.

Voice – person or character whom we imagine 'speaking' a poem, which may or may not simply be the poet speaking as himself or herself.

Answers

Pages 4–9: How to Approach a Poem

QUICK TEST

1. The subject is what it appears to be about; themes are the ideas it explores (e.g. love or conflict).

2. Metre

3. Simile

EXAM PRACTICE

The first stanza sets the scene for the speaker's time of 'blissful dreams' but does not yet reveal what she wishes she could see when awake. Alliteration connects and emphasises 'blissful' and 'bless'. Stanza 2 focuses on hearing, revealing that she desires contact with a lost loved one. The final stanza touches on the 'cold' reality, but gives a sense of completion and hope by returning to the 'bliss' and 'dreams' of the opening stanza.

Pages 10–13: What is it About? How Subject Relates to Theme

QUICK TEST

1. Swinging

2. Textual evidence, in the form of a short quotation or reference.

3. Possible themes: childhood, innocence, loss.

4. She seems to be uneasy, fearful, feeling abandoned because her mother is too far away to hear. Shadows suggest threat.

EXAM PRACTICE

The girl is 'very scared' at the start, and then full of menacing 'whisperings' of fears. This changes to excitement in the middle stanzas, in which her leaping heart could signify both exhilaration and nervousness. The repetition of 'fourth time' slows the poem down, as if she is relishing the memory. In the final two stanzas, however, a sense of threat returns and grows, with the girl left alone, feeling 'small', still swinging but abandoned, with shadows all around.

Pages 14–18: What is it About? Narrative Poems

QUICK TEST

1. (b) and (c)

2. Structure

3. It emphasises his car being stuck in traffic for what seems like a very long time.

EXAM PRACTICE

In the sudden silence after his lawnmower has stalled, the narrator has heard a sound that he cannot identify but which comes to represent something mysteriously significant. His personification of 'inanimate objects' being surprised seems to describe his own sudden experience of them as if he were absent himself. He seems disturbed by the 'portentous' nature of the noise, unsettled, as if the world could collapse without explanation, like the 'books that crash' as if pushed by an invisible hand.

Pages 19–22: Voice, Viewpoint, Tone and Mood

QUICK TEST

1. 'My countrymen Kiltartan's poor' shows that the airman is an Irishman from a poor, rural background.

2. It is addressed to 'you', which presents a direct threat to the reader.

3. 'Love has no pride'

EXAM PRACTICE

The airman regards his death as his inevitable 'fate', and is unconcerned about when or where it will happen: it will just be 'somewhere' in the vagueness of 'the clouds above'. His simple language in 'Those that I fight ...' suggests that he is, ironically for an airman, a down-to-earth character, who has no passion or patriotism. However, he is sensitive to the fact that the condition of the poor will be unchanged by the war. Nothing will 'bring them loss / Or leave them happier'. He did not join up for conventional reasons, such as 'law' or 'duty'. Rather, he felt his future was a 'waste of breath' and was moved by an 'impulse' to fly.

Pages 23–27: Viewpoint, or Perspective

QUICK TEST

1. He, she, it, they

2. Stanza 1 describes the speaker's feelings of joy, using similes of nature. In stanza 2 she sees herself as elevated by happiness to the status of royalty, and orders all the trappings of that status. Stanza 2 is based on details of luxury, rather than on similes.

3. Present tense is likely to make it seem more immediate.

4. It suggests a lack of emotional warmth in the occupants of the house.

EXAM PRACTICE

The absence of sunlight implies a lack of emotional warmth. The adjectives 'arid' and 'barren' imply that the home is not emotionally sustaining. The lack of music symbolises a lack of joy. The sibilance of 'slippered' and 'surreptitiously' creates a sense of the visitors feeling they have to creep silently through the house. The arresting image of joy 'held tight in a fist' implies emotional constraint, even a threat of violence. It is ironic that the cellophane covers (probably on furniture) and foil on the cooker fail to prevent dust and grime collecting: their effort is wasted.

Pages 28–31: Tone and Mood

QUICK TEST

1. Tone is the poet's style of address, especially relating to level of formality, but including, for example, sadness, anger, humour and cynicism. Mood is the emotional effect of a poem or part of it.

2. Strongly emotional poems.

3. Informal language, rhyme, formal language used ironically, onomatopoeia.

4. There is a sudden change in the final stanza to a dragging rhythm, exaggerated by alliteration, suggesting an old man 'faltering forward' uncertainly, or without hope or enthusiasm.

EXAM PRACTICE

Although the poet is addressing a lost love, the first two stanzas are buoyed up by the thought that he can hear her voice. The strong, regular **dactylic** rhythm reflects this. In the second stanza he even imagines he can see her, with the visual detail of her gown raising the mood. However, the rhythm slows in the third stanza with the awkward rhyme of 'listlessness' and 'wistlessness', and harsh reality is suggested by the apathetic breeze and the wet meadow, and the idea that the woman is 'dissolved'. However, the real change comes in the final stanza, with its dragging rhythm, exaggerated by alliteration, suggesting an old man 'faltering forward' uncertainly, without hope or enthusiasm, and the details of the autumn leaves and north wind.

Pages 32–35: Forms

QUICK TEST

1. Iambic (one unstressed and stressed syllable).

2. A metre consisting of five units of syllables – usually iambic (so, five pairs of syllables).

3. A repeated unit of rhythm, e.g. an iambic foot is one pair of syllables.

4. If writing in a metre, they choose an appropriate one, and vary it for effect.

EXAM PRACTICE

The first four stanzas are in a regular iambic rhythm, with the short lines of trimeter often sounding childlike – as in 'My skirt flew off the world.' Then 'The fourth time, Oh, the fourth time' forces a break, with 'Oh' creating a sense of longing for that happy time. However, the change to a dragging trochaic rhythm in the fifth stanza creates a change of mood, accentuated by

the two-syllable rhymes of ringing–swinging and calling–falling. The effect is to make the mood less childlike and more ominous.

Pages 36–39: Structure

QUICK TEST

1. A metre is often repeated with each new stanza.

2. It tells a story – its structure is narrative.

3. Present tense: emphasises how the present moment drags the speaker back to the past, which then overwhelms his experience of the present – the concert.

4. Octave (8 lines) and sestet (6 lines).

EXAM PRACTICE

The poem is a Shakespearean sonnet, a form which often addresses the beloved, as this one does. It first refers to 'a wasted time' – perhaps when the lover is absent. The speaker then states the paradox that, in his absence, she is only fully alive when asleep. The rhyme scheme emphasises this by linking 'sleep' with 'keep'. The sense of paradox is strengthened by the pun in 'come awake. In the wake …', in which 'wake' means the aftermath of the lover's presence. She goes on to ask that she be able to hold his memory 'all night through'. The poem becomes more dreamlike with the image of the lover holding oranges, reaching a sensual climax in the image of her kissing the colour of his mouth. The last four lines explain her eagerness to fall asleep. The final couplet delivers a typical twist: the dreamed memory of the lover turns even darkness to light.

Pages 40–43: Language

QUICK TEST

1. Childlike, naïve.

2. It suggests that his memories are seductive – both attractive and unreliable.

3. Symbolism is the use of a material thing (as opposed to an idea) to represent an idea, e.g. a dove representing peace.

4. It implies that bell ringing is productive work, not just a pastime.

EXAM PRACTICE

The poet compares pulling the bell ropes to 'milking', which suggests that it is like a farmer pulling on the udders of a cow. However, it also suggests getting something nourishing and pure by doing this, perhaps even the 'milk of human kindness'. There is also a pun in 'strain', referring both to effort and music. 'Raucous tintinnabulation' is an interesting choice, the adjective and onomatopoeic noun implying a noisy clanging rather than beautiful music, reflecting 'complaints and grievances' rather than praise.

Pages 44–48: Imagery

QUICK TEST

1. A simile.
2. Using the image of a person or god to represent an idea, e.g. 'Old Father Time', or Cupid for love.
3. As the commander of an army.
4. It describes the bird in terms of a jet plane.

EXAM PRACTICE

The lake's stillness is captured in 'willow mirror': it reflects the trees overhanging it. The float being 'lipstick red' describes its bright colour and hints at its shape. Both this and 'antenna' suggest the human world incongruously entering the natural, the latter also suggesting, nonetheless, an invisible connection between the two. The 'fingerprint' simile carries on the idea of the lake's stillness, as well as suggesting the delicate, unsuspecting touch of the fish causing the ripple.

Pages 49–53: Sound Effects

QUICK TEST

1. 'kneel' and 'night'; by some definitions also 'lovelessness'.
2. It can connect the meanings of words, or contrast them. It can also create a sense of harmony.
3. Assonance. A rhyme is created by a repeated vowel sound and consonant, but with a different consonant sound following it. So, 'floor' and 'pour' rhyme because the vowel sounds and endings are the same.
4. Onomatopoeia.

EXAM PRACTICE

The word 'rain' occurs seven times in the poem – three times in the first line, and again coupled with 'rains'. This emphasises the constancy of the rain, and the way it dominates the speaker's thoughts. His 'solitude' is also emphasised by repetition. Sounds shape meaning throughout the poem, such as the dead 'd' sounds of 'solitude', 'blessed' (pronounced as two syllables) and 'dead' itself. Another example is the alliteration and assonance in 'still and stiff', the repeated sound reflecting the identical form of the 'Myriads' of reeds.

Pages 54–57: Comparing Poems

QUICK TEST

1. The poetic methods used to create meaning in the poem.
2. The exact question (i.e. not just all aspects of both poems).
3. In both, music triggers emotionally evocative memories. Both use water imagery for emotion.

4. 'Piano' focuses on the speaker's loss of childhood happiness, 'Long Ago' on a childhood memory of someone else's loss.

EXAM PRACTICE

- Both focus on childhood memories, but SGS ('A Small Girl Swinging') covers memories, numbered 1–4, then comes into the present.
- SGS narrator may still be a child, suggested by, e.g. 'tummy jiggled'; LA ('Long Ago') narrated by adult looking back ('when I was young').
- SGS moves from past tense to threatening present tense; LA narrates incident in past tense, then moves into present to indicate the song's effect.
- SGS ends on note of threat – absent mother and 'shadows'; LA ends with image of overwhelming weather and ocean.

Pages 58-62: Writing a Comparison

QUICK TEST

1. Comparing similarities and differences for one aspect within one paragraph, then doing the same in subsequent paragraphs.
2. They show the reader how your argument progresses, making connections between ideas, highlighting your comparison.
3. The first stanza narrates the incident, using past tense; the second uses present tense to describe how the speaker is now affected by the song.
4. 'Piano' is all in the present tense; 'Long Ago' shifts from past to present.

EXAM PRACTICE

'Piano' describes the unfolding memories receding to the point of childhood as a 'vista', suggesting a landscape over which the speaker gazes. The only other strongly visual detail is the 'great black piano', which suggests an unfavourable comparison between a full-size grand piano and a small upright one. 'Long Ago' is more visual, focusing on the memory of an old man and a rocking-horse glimpsed through 'a partly opened door'. The speaker associates the song with this visual memory.

Pages 72–73: Grade 7+ Comparison

EXAM PRACTICE

The Grade 5 comparison makes some good points but lacks sufficient explanation and evidence, and could explore the effects of imagery. The Grade 7+ comparison is more detailed, more insightful, and is more successful in analysing effects, especially of structure and imagery. It also uses more terminology, always accurately, and with an analysis of effects, especially in the final paragraph.